JESSICA SANDERS

22 Ways to Make Extra Money

Copyright © 2019 by Jessica Sanders

All rights reserved. No part of this publication may be reproduced, stored or transmitted in any form or by any means, electronic, mechanical, photocopying, recording, scanning, or otherwise without written permission from the publisher. It is illegal to copy this book, post it to a website, or distribute it by any other means without permission.

Jessica Sanders asserts the moral right to be identified as the author of this work.

Jessica Sanders has no responsibility for the persistence or accuracy of URLs for external or third-party Internet Websites referred to in this publication and does not guarantee that any content on such Websites is, or will remain, accurate or appropriate.

Designations used by companies to distinguish their products are often claimed as trademarks. All brand names and product names used in this book and on its cover are trade names, service marks, trademarks and registered trademarks of their respective owners. The publishers and the book are not associated with any product or vendor mentioned in this book. None of the companies referenced within the book have endorsed the book.

First edition

This book was professionally typeset on Reedsy.
Find out more at reedsy.com

Contents

INTRODUCTION	1
AMAZON FBA	2
BECOME A SILENT PARTNER	6
BUY AND SELL DOMAINS	9
BUY EXISTING BUSINESS	15
BUY ROYALTIES	23
CAR WASH	31
CASHBACK REWARDS CARD	40
CREATE BUSINESS SYSTEM & FRANCHISE IT OUT	43
DROPSHIPPING	49
EBATES	54
ECOMMERCE	56
GET PAID TO HAVE AN APP ON YOUR PHONE	63
GOOGLE ADSENSE	69
LAUNDROMAT	76
ONLINE ARBITRAGE	83
RESELL ON EBAY	90
START A BLOG OR BUY A BLOG	96
STORAGE RENTALS	103
TAX LIEN CERTIFICATES	106
VENDING MACHINE	109
YOUTUBE CHANNEL	112
Final Words	122

INTRODUCTION

If you are looking for ways to make extra money, this book will get your creative juices to rolling. There are 22 ways of making extra money mention in this book, hopefully at least one will work for you. Some of the ideas mention in this book involve offline methods as well as online methods for generating extra income.

AMAZON FBA

The Fulfillment by Amazon (FBA) business model continues to grow in popularity, and for good reason. Fundamentally, it's the same as a traditional e-commerce business. But, instead of you having to fulfill orders one by one, Amazon stores your products for you and even picks, packs and ships them out to customers on your behalf.

This makes it an lot easier for you to build your business without having to worry about the logistics of warehouses, packaging materials, couriers and so on. With private labeling, you also have the opportunity to build your own brand and website, thereby increasing the value of your business.

Ready to go? Here's a basic guide for starting an FBA business.

What Is Fulfillment by Amazon?

The FBA business model allows you to leverage Amazon's robust distribution network and customer base. As noted, Amazon will warehouse your products, fulfill orders and even provide customer service so you don't have to be hands-on with every aspect of the business. What this means for entrepreneurs is that you can act like a big corporation without the headache of actually being one. You can focus on finding product opportunities while Amazon handles the rest on your behalf.

In a typical ecommerce business, you have to figure out the logistics of sending products to your customers in a timely manner. However, with FBA, Prime members get most orders shipped to their door within two to five days. Another common challenge with an ecommerce store is that inventorying and listing additional products for sale can increase the complexity of your business.

With FBA, all you need to do is ship the products to Amazon's warehouse, and the company will take over from there. You can easily increase your product selection without significantly adding to your workload.

Create an Amazon seller account.

First things first: In order to get your FBA business up and running, you're going to need to create an Amazon seller account. Go to Amazon's website, scroll down to the footer and look for the heading marked "Make Money with Us." Then, click on the link that reads "Sell on Amazon."

At this point, you can either sign up as an "Individual" or a "Professional." When you sign up as an "Individual," you will not be charged a monthly subscription fee. If you're looking to build a business over the long haul, then you'll want to sign up as a "Professional." The first-month is free, and after that, it's $39.99 per month plus selling fees.

Other than that, the signup process is relatively straightforward. Follow the onscreen instructions and complete setup.

Uncover product opportunities and establish your private label.

There are a number of different ways to leverage the FBA model, but the most popular way is private labeling. The idea is to establish a brand or label, apply it to your product and sell it on Amazon.

First, you will need to do your Amazon product research. This is the most important step for a variety of reasons. If you enter an unpopular product category and sell a product for more than your competition is selling it for, you could lose money on that product. If you take the time to find a popular product category, do competitive analysis, study product reviews and identify a product that you can improve upon or sell at a better price, you'll have found the sweet spot.

Another popular way to sell products through Amazon is with retail arbitrage — buying a brand name product and flipping it on Amazon for profit. This is a much easier way of making money on Amazon, at least in the short term. With private labeling, you need capital. Ordering private label products may cost you several thousand dollars, but if you're looking to build an asset that can later be sold, then this is the direction you want to go in.

Another key piece of the puzzle is your supplier. You can't make money if you don't have products in stock, so you need to ensure that the time delay between the placement and delivery of the order is as short as it can possibly be.

Tips for growing and scaling your FBA business
- Pursue your passion. If you enjoy doing it, you will stick with it for longer. Find a product category that interests and excites you.
- Increase your product offerings. You will need to do proper research for every new product offering you create. Having more products can reduce the risk of your business becoming dependent on just one product.
- Improve your Best Sellers Rank. BSR is an important metric for both your customers and your sales. This is also a key factor when the time comes to sell your business. Buyers will want to see steady

growth in your BSR rank over time.
- Build your brand website. As you continue to expand your private label product offerings, you'll want to build a professional, dedicated site for your business. This gives you another way to market your products, and can also make your business attractive to potential buyers.
- Become an Amazon Associate. Increase your revenues by becoming an affiliate with Amazon. Refer customers to your products from your own site, and start earning commissions.

Earning potential

How much do FBA business owners earn? What is the earning potential of an FBA business?

Spencer Haws from Niche Pursuits reports he was able to make nearly $40,000 within 30 days of starting his FBA business. Chris Guthrie from UpFuel made almost $3,000 within 30 days. James Amazio, founder of Feedbackz, went from zero to $50,000 per month in just eight months.

These results aren't necessarily typical, but they do show that it is possible to build a five-, six- or even seven-figure business by leveraging the FBA model.

Final thoughts

Although starting an FBA business will require up-front capital, the effort will be nowhere near as intensive as it would be with a traditional ecommerce business. Getting your business off the ground is the easy part. Finding ways to grow your FBA business is the more difficult part. Take advantage of the resources available to you, and systematize your processes as you go. Signup for Amazon Fba (https://amzn.to/2S6BYTb)

BECOME A SILENT PARTNER

Many business savvy individuals have considered the thought of becoming a silent partner at one point or another in their careers. The thought of investing in a lucrative business and sharing in the profits without any additional effort is an attractive proposition to seriously contemplate. Basically, a silent partner is an individual who invests capital into a business in exchange for a share in the profits or losses of that business.

Silent partners are not supposed to have a role in the day-to-day operation of the business, and that is where the term 'silent' originates from. They do, however, have a say in anything that affects the management of the company because management and its choice of direction is the reason for the partnership in the first place.

Benefits of a Silent Partnership

There are several benefits that are available to a silent partner that do not exist for other members of the business. Silent partners have little to no responsibility when it comes to the operation of the business on a daily level. Silent partners are brought into a company because of their financial resources, not their knowledge of operations of the company.

Perhaps the main reason individuals become silent partners is the ability to enjoy a passive income stream without having to constantly monitor an investment. The essential basis of a silent partnership is trust in the individual or group that is running the business.

Once trust in the capabilities and direction of the company is established, there is little other responsibility for a silent partner other than to enjoy the profits generated by the company. The key to being a successful silent partner is to completely evaluate all aspects of the company prior to committing to the investment. It is vital to establish the trust needed to limit involvement in the company and act like a silent partner.

Things Can Go Wrong

Not every silent partnership works out as intended, even when all the research has been done prior to the agreement. Even the most brilliantly managed companies can come up against issues that might hinder their growth or cause unseen difficulties.

When these situations arise, the common instinct for silent partners who have large amounts of capital invested in a company is to overreact and attempt to involve themselves in the operational aspects of the company in order to correct the situation. This can lead to difficult situations where the silent partner oversteps the boundaries of their role in the partnership and creates a dysfunctional scenario in the operation of the company.

Importance of the Partnership Agreement

Perhaps the most important aspect of becoming a silent partner is to have strict limits of involvement detailed in the partnership agreement. Preventing silent investors from interfering in the daily operations of a faltering company is vital to preventing the possible damage that can occur when the investor involves themselves out of a financial panic.

This is where trust in the direction and capabilities of the management team become so vital to the success of the partnership arrangement. It is important also for the silent partner and the company to have an exit strategy in place should the relationship move in a direction that neither party is happy with.

This can be a buyout clause on the part of the company or some form of loss mitigation stipulation for the investor that can be detailed in the partnership agreement. Ultimately, if all parties know the boundaries prior to the agreement and abide by them, trouble can usually be avoided should things not go as planned.

Conclusion

Becoming a silent partner can be an excellent investment opportunity for individuals when the right situation presents itself. As long as the investor spends the time to thoroughly research the company's historical business record as well as their management staff and business philosophy, investing as a silent partner can be a safe and lucrative investment strategy.

Companies with proven track records can be difficult for investors to get involved with because they usually do not require outside financing, but if the opportunity presents itself, the investor should act decisively. Becoming a silent partner is not for everyone, but for those who are comfortable with a hands-off approach to business investing, becoming a silent partner can be a rewarding and lucrative enterprise.

BUY AND SELL DOMAINS

Buying and selling domain names is an exciting adventure that for some seems to conjure up images of finding hidden pirate treasure or guessing the winning combination on the next Powerball. Stories abound of domains that were purchased for $8 dollars 15 years ago being sold today for millions. Of course, that leads the more adventurous of us to wonder, "How can I do that?"

Well, the ocean is big. Your likelihood of cashing in on the motherlode is low, and you're liable to waste a lot of time and money chasing after the wrong ships. You need a map or some other advantage to guide you toward success.

5 tips for buying and selling domain names for profit

Here are some tips to get you pointed in the right direction when trying to buy or sell a domain name for profit:
- Narrow your focus.
- Find names that offer real value.
- Check domain availability.
- Evaluate the price.
- Get your domains front and center.

Let's dig into each of these tips.

1. *Narrow your focus*

Buying and Selling Domains Narrow Focus Map

There are millions of domains already registered by someone and endless combinations of available domains to register, especially when you consider the hundreds of new domain name extensions like .app and .club. If you plan on buying a domain to resell it, you should start by narrowing your focus.

What do you know about already that can make this easier? Do you know about pets? Are you in car or home sales? Do you know about education or healthcare? Think about some of the spaces you are most familiar with and start there.

Here's what you DON'T want to do: Target prospective buyers based on their perceived economic status, without any insight into the industry you're targeting. "Lawyers seem to do well," you think, "maybe I should start selling names to them." So you rush out and buy a bunch of domain names you think would appeal to the law firms you've identified as potential buyers.

Without knowledge of the space, you may not know that the American Bar Association and other industry-specific organizations set rules that govern some aspects of legal advertising. You're not going to strike gold selling names your target buyers can't use.

Remember to focus on the areas you know well and you will be much more successful than buying domains you think would benefit someone in an industry you know little about.

2. *Find names that offer real value*

Think of ways that the domains you buy would be a valuable asset to the buyer. Picture someone who would benefit from buying the domain in a space you are very familiar with. If this was you and someone was trying to sell you this name, would it be beneficial for you to own? Be honest. If so, why? If not, why?

Let's play this out with a real example. Say you're familiar with the real estate market in Tempe, Arizona, and you have the opportunity to purchase tempeapartments.com for $200. This might be a good deal. Tempe has a lot of rental property; it's a competitive market; and there's ample turnover in the apartment space because the city is home to a major university. Ask yourself:

- How much does one month of rent profit a landlord, property manager or other prospective domain buyer? How about a year's worth of rental profit?
- Would you buy this name if you were in the space? If so, why?
- What kind of domains are landlords, property managers, etc., using?
- How much do they spend on advertising?
- How much would this domain help them to sound authoritative in their space?

If you can answer these questions with confidence and know this niche well, you probably already have an idea of who to contact and how to make a compelling case for how this domain could help their business grow.

Related: This entrepreneur spent $900,000 on great.com — Is a premium domain worth the investment?

3. *Check domain availability*

Now that you have narrowed down what names you should probably be buying, how do you find them?

If the names are taken (as many probably will be), head over to the aftermarket to buy from people who already own the names or who let them expire because they no longer plan on using them. A great place to look is auctions.godaddy.com. Use the advanced search option to quickly hone in on the type of names you are interested in.

You can narrow the results by price, top-level domain (i.e, .com, .net, .org, .club, etc.), keyword, and many more filters. Using this feature will help you quickly sort through the millions of domains on the aftermarket and find the domain names that best fit your end goals.

4. Evaluate the price

Once you have a name in mind, how do you know if the price is fair? I like to use namebio.com to compare the domain I'm thinking about buying with similar domains that have sold. You can enter the keyword and also use some advanced search features to see a list of names similar to yours, what they actually sold for, and when they sold.

You can also research current domain sales on venues like GoDaddy Auctions and Afternic. Finally, Ron Jackson issues a weekly report on DN Journal that covers the top public sales of the week. You can use all these resources to help you price your domains correctly.

A great place to look is auctions.godaddy.com.

Use the advanced search option to quickly hone in on the type of names you are interested in. You can narrow the results by price, top-level domain (i.e, .com, .net, .org, .club, etc.), keyword, and many more filters.

Using this feature will help you quickly sort through the millions of domains on the aftermarket and find the domain names that best fit your end goals.

5. Get your domains front and center

There are many venues to get your domains out in front of the buying public. You want to consider a few things:

Is the venue trusted and well known?

It's important to feel confident that you will get paid and that the buyer will get the domain name they paid for. Pick a place that has good ratings with recognized bodies such as the Better Business Bureau or licensing from a trusted government source. This will make it easier for the buyer to pull the trigger on the domain purchase as well knowing they can trust the brand that is selling the domain. A trusted brand is vital when selling a domain.

Is the distribution network strong?

The potential to get your domain name in front of the right buyer is key. Listing in a distribution network such as Afternic can get your domain name in front of millions of potential buyers each month.

Do you know people who could benefit from the domain name? Why not reach out to them and see if they have any interest in using the domain? If you are working in an area of the domain space you are familiar with you should be able to convey the value proposition of your domain name for the potential buyer.

You do not want to start sending spam emails. You want to have conversations with people you know would appreciate the ability to own the domain. Letting a great name you purchased at a fair price to make a profit sit in your account, instead of getting it in front of the right buyer, is like finally finding that pirate treasure map but framing it to admire in your living room instead of following it to the booty.

Resources to learn more

There is always a learning curve in buying domains with the purpose of reselling them. Don't hesitate to ask a lot of questions to those who went before you, participate in forums such as namepros.com, keep abreast of industry trends via resources like domaining.com, and reach out to the Afternic and GoDaddy Aftermarket support teams.

Attend a conference. By doing so you will really ramp up your knowledge quickly and meet a lot of other professionals who are in the industry. You can also see first hand the tools and services available to you from various vendors in the space. All of these things will help you to be a smarter investor and make the most of your time and money.

BUY EXISTING BUSINESS

Buying a company that's already established may be quicker and easier than starting from scratch. However, you will need to put time and effort into finding the business that's right for you. Also, the costs involved in buying a existing business can be substantial and should not be underestimated.

This guide takes you through the steps of buying an existing business, including how to assess and value a business and your obligations to any existing staff.

Advantages and disadvantages of buying a business

There can be many good reasons why buying an existing business could make good business sense. Remember though, that you will be taking on the legacy of the previous business owner. You need to be aware of every aspect of the business you're about to buy.

Advantages
- Some of the groundwork to get the business up and running will have been done
- It may be easier to obtain finance as the business will have a proven track record
- A market for the product or service will have already been demonstrated
- There may be established customers, a reliable income and a

reputation to capitalise and build on. There will be a useful network of contacts
- A business plan and marketing method should already be in place
- Existing employees should have experience you can draw on
- Many of the problems will have been discovered and solved already

Disadvantages
- You often need to invest a large amount up front, and will also have to budget for professional fees for solicitors, surveyors, accountants etc
- You will probably also need several months' worth of working capital to assist with cash flow
- For an neglected business you may need to invest more on top of the purchase price to give it the best chance of success
- You may need to honour or renegotiate any outstanding contracts the previous owner leaves
- You also need to consider why the current owner is selling up. Think about how this might impact the business and you're taking it over
- Current staff may not be happy with an new boss, or the business might have been run badly and staff morale may be low

Decide on the business to buy

Any business you buy needs to fit your own skills, lifestyle and aspirations. Before you start looking, think about what you can bring to a business and what you'd like to get back. List what is important to you. Look at your motivations and what you ultimately want to achieve.

It is useful to consider:
- Your abilities – can you achieve what you want to achieve?
- Your capital – how much money do you have to invest?
- Your expectations in terms of earning – what level of profit do you

need to be looking for to accommodate your needs?
- Your commitment - are you prepared for all the hard work and money that you will need to put into the business to get it to succeed?
- Your strengths - what kind of business opportunity will give you the chance to put your skills and experience to good use?
- The business sector you're interested in - learn as much as you can about your chosen industry so you can compare different businesses. It's important to take the time to talk to people already in similar businesses. The internet and your local library will also be good sources of information
- Location - don't restrict your search to your local area. Some businesses can be easily relocated

How to value a business

There are several valuation methods you can use to value a business. Your accountant may be able to help. However, a business transfer agent, business broker or corporate-financier will be best qualified to provide valuation advice.

Look at:
- the history of the business
- its current performance - sales, turnover, profit
- future projections or a business plan
- its financial situation - cashflow, debts, expenses, assets
- why the business is being sold
- any outstanding or major litigation the business is involved in
- any regulatory changes which might have an impact on the business

Talk to the vendor and, if possible, the business' existing customers and suppliers. The vendor must be comfortable with you doing this and you must be sensitive to their position. Customer and suppliers may be able to give you information that affects your valuation, as well as information about market conditions affecting the business.

For example, if the vendor is being forced to sell due to decreasing profits, your valuation might be lower.

Intangible assets

Valuing the intangible assets is usually difficult and could include:
- the company's reputation
- the relationship with suppliers
- the value of goodwill
- the value of licences
- patents or intellectual property
- Other factors that will affect the value:
- stock
- location
- assets
- products
- debtors
- creditors
- suppliers
- employees
- premises
- competition
- benchmarking - what other businesses in the sector have sold for
- who else in the sector is for sale or on the market
- the economic climate - will any new government legislation have an impact on the business

Due diligence

Once an offer has been made and accepted a period of time is allowed for you to access the business' books and records. This is known as due diligence. It should give you a realistic picture of how the business is performing now, and how it is likely to perform in the future. It should also highlight any issues or problems which might need warranting or guaranteeing.

There are traditionally three types of due diligence. You might need different advisors for each:
- legal due diligence – as part of a sales and purchase contract, the lawyers can check that the business has legal title to sell, ownership of all the assets and that regulatory and litigation issues are fully addressed
- financial due diligence – checking the numbers and making sure there are no black holes or hidden financial issues
- commercial due diligence – finding out the business' place in the marketplace, checking competitors and the regulatory environment

Don't start due diligence until you have agreed a price and terms with the seller. They may agree to take the business off the market during your investigation. This is known as an exclusivity period and the seller will often ask for a down payment to secure it. The investigation period is negotiable – but most small businesses need at least three to four weeks.

Where to get help

Ideally, you should get accountants and solicitors to help you identify risk areas. If it is registered with Companies House, you can also obtain copies of the company accounts, the annual return and the other key documents.

Due diligence is about more than the finances of a business. You need to know exactly what you are getting into, what needs to be fixed, what it will cost to fix, and if you are the right person to take on this business.

Key areas to cover are:
- employment terms and conditions
- outstanding litigation
- major contracts and orders
- IT systems and other technology
- environmental issues
- commercial management including customer service, research and development, and marketing
- You may also need information from external sources such as the landlord, tax office or bank.

Buying a business
- A organised approach will help you find and acquire the right business.
- Get professional advice
- Professional help is invaluable as you go through the negotiation, valuation and purchase process.

Research

Research the sector you're interested in, including the best time to buy, and shortlist two or three businesses.

Initial viewing and valuation

Be discreet – the owner may not want staff to know they are selling, but be thorough and record key findings.

Arrange finance

Lenders generally require:
- details of the business/sales particulars
- accounts for the last three years
- financial projections – if no accounts are available
- details of your personal assets and liabilities

Make a formal offer

If you make your initial offer by phone, follow this up in writing. Head your letter 'subject to contract' and include this phrase in all written communication.

Negotiation

Before completing the sale, it may be worth trying to negotiate an overlap period so you have time to become familiar with the business before taking over. You and your solicitor need to verify the information you have based your offer on. If you're buying premises, you may want to arrange an independent survey and valuation, even if a lender is also carrying out their own survey and valuation at your expense.

Completion

Even after you reach an agreement on the price and terms of sale, the deal could still fall through. You have to meet certain conditions of sale to complete, including:
- verification of financial statements
- transfer of leases
- transfer of contracts/licences
- transfer of finance
- transfer of existing or new VAT registration

Looking after existing employees

There are regulations that govern what happens to employees when someone new takes over a business. These apply to all employees when a business is transferred as a going concern. This means employees automatically start working for the new owner under the same terms and conditions.

Employment tribunal awards

When you buy an existing business, you might decide you need to employ fewer staff. But be careful about making any changes, as an employee might take a case to an employment tribunal for unfair dismissal or unfair selection for redundancy. It's best to consult a solicitor before making any such changes.

Inform and consult employees

You may want to discuss reducing employee numbers or reorganising staff. However, it's a good idea to wait until you have completed the due diligence period, but before you take over the business. As the new employer you should inform and consult all employees - including employee representatives - who may be affected.

Pensions

As their new employer, you do not have to take over rights and obligations relating to employees' occupational pension schemes put in place by the previous employer. However, if you don't provide comparable pensions arrangements, you could theoretically face a claim for unfair dismissal.

BUY ROYALTIES

Dolly Parton is still collecting royalties from her song, "I Will Always Love You."

It was originally recorded in 1973 and was #1 Billboard country song in 1974 and 1982. Then Whitney Houston covered it for the movie The Bodyguard in 1992 and it reached the #1 spot again and became one of the best-selling singles of all time.

Wouldn't it be amazing to be able to collect royalties on songs like these, forever?

Even if you've never written a song, you can still collect on royalties. If you're looking for an alternative investment opportunity, royalties are worth looking at.

While stock prices constantly fluctuate, royalty revenues have continued to grow.

According to the International Confederation of Societies of Authors and Composers, in 2008 the 2.5 million artists represented by the group collected over seven billion dollars in royalties. Now You Can Collect Royalties for Songs You Didn't Even Write

How is it possible?

There are times when an artist who owns the royalties for a song, and they would rather have some of the money right now. Maybe they want to buy a house, or build their business, or cover immediate living expenses. Investors who want to have a stable income stream can buy a percentage of those royalties on The Royalty Exchange.

The Royalty Exchange is the #1 marketplace for buying and selling royalties. The company was founded in 2011, and they have auctions and even IPO's on music catalogs like pre-2013 Eminem.

The owner of the royalties puts their work up for auction, with a minimum bid that they will accept. Once the royalties are purchased, the organizations that pay the royalties put the money into an escrow account and the royalties are then paid every quarter or every six months. Buyers get a dashboard where they can keep track of their purchases and earnings.

For example, someone bought 25% of the royalties for the 1984 Alabama song, "If You're Gonna Play in Texas," for $56,000. The website shows that that song earned $4,992 in royalties over the past 12 months. The royalties for an album of worship music was sold for $122,000. That album earned $20,190 in royalties over the past 12 months. Sometimes the royalties are auctioned off by a collaborator of the song, or by someone who has inherited the royalty rights.

According to an article called, "Are Music Royalties a New Alternative Investment?" by John Waggoner in Investment News, Tony Geiss, the songwriter for a collection of Sesame Street songs including "Elmo's World" gave his share of the royalties to charity. His estate auctioned them off for $580,000 so that the charities could benefit from the gift immediately.

Royalties can go up because a song was used in a soundtrack or because one of the artists died. Royalties for songs are not correlated to the stock market, which is a big draw for investors.

Get Started on These Platforms

The Royalty Exchange is an online royalty marketplace where you can bid on royalties in many industries such as music, film, TV, books, solar energy, pharmaceutical, intellectual property, oil, gas and more. You pay a 2.5% buyer premium and another 2.5% for the management and payout of your royalty stream.

Lyric Financial is another royalty platform to try. Lyric Financial is a company created to help musicians have the money they need to finance their careers and pay the bills. They give musicians short-term advances on their all or a portion of their royalties. They also offer lines of credit to musicians who earn $100,000 or more a year in royalties.

SongVest describes themselves as the stock market of music. Through their website, you can buy or sell royalties. Fans can finance albums that are being made now through a crowdfunding model, and in return get a percentage of the royalties. The money raised allows the musicians to create and market the albums.

How Can You Tell if a Song Will Earn a Lot of Money?

According to an article on The Royalty Exchange, the most important factor in how much money a song makes is how often it is used. The more popular the song is, the more it is played, and the more money it will make. In addition to popularity, holiday songs make a lot of money over a long period of time because they are played over and over every year.

If a song is used in a soundtrack to a movie, it will earn more royalties.

And when a song is covered and reinterpreted by a new artist, both the original artist and the new artist will earn royalties.

The top ten highest earning songs are "Candle in the Wind," by Elton John and Bernie Taupin; "The Christmas Song," by Mel Torme and Bob Wells; "Pretty Woman" by Roy Orbison and Bill Dees; "Every Breath You Take," by Sting; "Santa Claus is Coming to Town" by Haven Gillespie and Fred J. Coots; "Stand By Me," by Ben E. King, Jerry Leiber and Mike Stoller; "Unchained Melody," by Alex North and Hy Zaret; "Yesterday" by John Lennon and Paul McCartney; "You've Lost That Feeling," by Barry Mann, Cynthia Weil and Phil Spector; and "White Christmas," by Irving Berlin.

Pension Funds are Increasing their Returns by Investing in Royalties

In his article, "Warren Buffett's Tollbooth Investment Strategy," Simon Black writes that most pension funds are seriously underfunded simply because they get a low return. When pension managers invest, they are looking for ways to get a safe return. Unfortunately, it's nearly impossible to get a safe return of more than 7-8%.

But royalties are different. Royalties can often bring in as much as 10-25% per year.

You are getting paid for other people to use an asset that you own. Warren Buffett compares owning royalties to owning a toll road. Once you build the road you can collect cash forever just for letting people use the road. For this reason, many pension fund managers have been adding royalties to their mix of assets as a way to safely boost their returns. The Canada Pension Plan Investment Board allocated $325 million for a percentage of the royalties in Venetoclax, a cancer drug.

Round Hill Music Royalty Fund owns rights to more than 4,000 songs, including Chris Kenner's Land of a Thousand Dances, which appears in the movie Forrest Gump. According to the CEO of Round Hill Music Royalty Fund, the song generates between $300,000-$400,000 a year.

The benefits of investing in royalties are that you can have a steady income that lasts for the lifetime of the copyright or patent, royalties are not influenced by the stock market and so they are a good way to diversify your portfolio, and there is always the possibility that your royalty will have a revenue spike.

You Can Invest in Royalties in Other Industries

What is a royalty? Whenever the owner of an asset is paid so that other people can use that asset, they are receiving a royalty. Aside from the entertainment industry, people can invest in royalties in oil, natural gas, and other minerals.

In her article, "Royalties as an Alternative Investment," Enelda Butler explained it this way: "The owner may license the asset to be used by another party, and will be paid a percentage of the net revenues of the asset based on its usage. Royalties can also be used to allow investors in a company to have a percentage ownership of future production or revenues that will be paid at specified intervals like annually, quarterly or monthly."

It's like owning an oil well without all the drilling.

Owning and operating an oil well is out of reach for most people. But you can get a percentage of all the revenue that comes from all that by investing in an oil and gas royalty trust. In "Energy Investing 101: Tackling Oil & Gas Royalty Trusts," Motley Fool writer Tyler Crowe provides a good primer for people who want to take advantage of these high-yield investments. Investing in a royalty trust is similar to buying the royalties to a song. The oil company will issue units of a royalty trust so that they can raise capital.

There are several reasons why these investments are worth including in your portfolio.
- They are corporate tax-exempt.
- The distributions count as capital gains, which have a lower tax rate.
- You will become a part owner, which means that you can lower your cost basis by depreciating the asset, delay your taxes and take advantage of tax credits.
- The ten largest oil and gas royalty trusts get returns that range from 8.4% to 28.5%. Royalty trusts are required to distribute all of their cash flow, which is why the yields are so high.

Oil and gas royalty trusts are more like bonds than trusts. They have a finite lifespan. Crowe said, "It's value slowly declines over time until it's no longer economically feasible to pull oil and gas from the well." The amount of the distributions vary depending on oil and gas prices, how much the wells are producing and other factors.

Although the yields may be high, there is no guarantee that you will earn back the principal. That said, some of the well-established trusts have beaten the S&P 500 for the past 15 years.

Before deciding to invest, the Motley Fool recommends looking at three things. 1) The production mix of the well; what percentage is oil, natural gas, etc. 2) The Payback period; the amount of time it will take to break even. 3) The shelf life of the trust; the total amount of time the trust will be in production.

Royalty Companies in the Mining Industry

In a Stansberry Research article called, "How to Make the Biggest Safest Returns Possible with Royalty Companies," John Doody, the editor of Gold Stock Analyst, explains the benefits of investing in royalty companies. One of the biggest benefits is that investing in royalty companies lets you enjoy the high returns from the precious metals mines without the risk that can come with mines.

"There's a lot of risk associated with a one- or two-mine company. It's common to see mines encounter difficulties for various reasons, and the related mining stocks might lose 25%, 50%, or more of their value in one day," said Doody. "On the other hand, if a big royalty company had a royalty on that mine, it wouldn't be a big deal, because there would be royalties from other mines that could take up the slack."

Royalties as a Form of Venture Capital Financing

epaCUBE was founded in Dallas, TX, in 2001. It is a SaaS company that provides profit optimization solutions.

They needed funding so that they could adjust their business model and fund new sales and marketing effort. To make this happen, they went to Cypress Growth Capital, who gave them $2 million in 2013.

Cypress offers royalty-based growth capital. The Cypress Growth Capital website said, "Unlike a traditional equity investment, extraordinary growth projections and market opportunity are not prerequisites for royalty-based growth capital. As a royalty investor, our investment success is not dependent on an exit event, like a sale of the company or a public stock offering."

Entrepreneurs and start-ups are turning to a royalty based model of capital funding, like the ones offered at Cypress. Normally, companies have to give up the control of their company and a chunk of equity whenever they receive funding from investors.

But with royalty-based financing, investors get a monthly payout based on the revenue of the company. Rather than get an ownership stake, investors get a guaranteed percentage of the sales. Royalty Capital Management, BDC Capital and Rockwater Capital are three investment firms that specialize in the royalty-based model.

Diversify Your Portfolio with Royalties

Investing in royalties is a good way to diversify your portfolio because it is possible to get a high return on your investment with relatively low risk. Musicians occasionally sell all or part of the royalties for their songs and albums, and investors can bid on them on several online marketplaces. Once you win a bid on a royalty, you will receive the royalty checks whenever that song is played. Many pension funds are turning to royalties as a way to increase their yields.

Other industries have opportunities to buy royalties. The oil and gas industry sells royalty rights through oil and gas royalty trusts. Many startups and small businesses are funded through royalty deals where the investor gets a percentage of the revenues that are coming in.

What do you think? Do royalties have a place in your portfolio?

CAR WASH

Opening a car wash business can be a fun, interesting, and profitable business for somebody with business smarts and perseverance. With the right location, good marketing, and top-notch service, you can draw in numerous customers who need their cars washed quickly, efficiently, and at a good price. However, opening a car wash business also requires a significant investment, good planning, and attention to detail in order to make your business profitable.

Part 1. Planning Your Car Wash

1. Research the car wash business. Even if you've worked at a car wash business, you'll need to be up to date on all the latest trends and technologies to have a good understanding of the industry. Visit other car washes and figure out the type of car wash you would like to open (e.g. self-service, automatic, waterless, full detailing, etc.)

For example, people use car washes more when the economy is doing well and when motor vehicle sales are up. When people have more money to spend, they are more willing to pay for a car wash. Knowing the car sales statistics in your area could help you predict success for your business.

- Talk to car wash owners, car wash suppliers, and car wash equipment manufacturers. You want to understand the car wash business from all sides so you know what you are getting into.

- Read Internet trend reports and business periodicals. Find out what the demographics are in your area and read up on how car wash businesses are doing in areas with similar demographics.
- Read business publications to find out what the newest materials and equipment are. The car wash industry is developing more energy efficient and environmentally friendly materials, so it's important to stay abreast of new developments.

2. Investigate the competition in your area. In order for your business to be competitive, you need to thoroughly research the other car washes in your area. If you have already chosen a location for your car wash, scope out all the competition within a 5 mile radius. What services do they offer? What is their prices? How do they market their business? How often are customers using the services?
- Take notes as you investigate the car washes. You can go back and review them as you make plans for your car wash.
- Also pay attention to the other businesses around the car washes. If a car wash has a high volume of customers, what are some of the factors that are contributing to this? Is it located in a busy shopping center or right off the highway?

3. Draw up a detailed business plan. A business plan will help you get financing to start your car wash and think through the details of your business. Make your plan as detailed as possible. The business plan should include an introduction (3-5 pages), market analysis (9-22 pages), company description (1-2 pages), organization and management (3-5 pages), marketing and sales strategies (4-6 pages), product/service (4-10 pages), equity investment and funding request (2-4 pages), financial information (12-25 pages).

- The introduction should include your Executive Summary, table of

contents, and a cover page.
- Your market analysis demonstrates your knowledge of the car wash industry and the results of any market research and analysis that you have done. Who are your customers and what are their purchasing habits? What are the risks, strengths, and weaknesses involved with opening a car wash? What is your projected revenue based on the current market and future market trends?
- Your company description should include information about your car wash business and why you think it will be successful.
- The organization and management section should detail the structure of your company, the board of directors, and the qualifications of your management team.
- The marketing and sales portion should clearly outline your marketing strategy. How will you get customers? What avenues will you use to reach them? What is your overall sales strategy?
- The product or service section outlines exactly what you will be selling. How does your car wash business fill a void in the market? Why would people want to use your car wash as opposed to other car washes?
- The equity and funding section details exactly how much money you will need to start your business and what financial resources you already have to invest in the business.
- The financial information is the most important part of your business plan and should be reviewed by an accountant or financial planner. Include your personal financial information, any existing businesses you have, a list of debts, projected income for 5 years, and certification that your information was reviewed by a 3rd party financial adviser.

4. Find the investment capital to open a car wash. You can finance your new car wash through bank financing, a Small Business Association (SBA) loan, or through private investors. You will also need to have

some cash of your own saved up to secure financing from others. The best way to do this is by presenting your business plan to your potential investor and show how your idea can be a viable business.
- A bank loan requires a loan-to-value ratio of 75%. You will need to come up with 25% of the fair market value and the bank will fund the other 75%. It will be harder for you to secure bank financing if you have never owned a business before.
- An SBA loan will either be a 7a or a 504. If you get a 7a loan, the SBA will partner with a local investor. Your actual loan will be financed by the local lender. A 504 loan is actually financed by the SBA and has job creation criteria.
- The start up costs for a car wash range from $100,000 - $400,000.

5. Choose the location for your car wash business. Having the right location can make or break your business. A successful location should be near a shopping center, in a high traffic, residential area, be easily and visible accessible from the road, allow for expansions and business growth, and have enough space for cars to line up.
- Your sign is visible to drivers for at least 40 seconds. Ideally, traffic should travel past at no more than 40 miles per hour (64 km/hr) so drivers have time to see your signage and make that split-second decision to have their cars washed.
- Choose a venue large enough to accommodate the bays, pump rooms, vacuum and drying areas, and the office.
- Check your city's zoning regulations to be sure you are allowed to open a car wash at your chosen location. If you need a special permit, obtain it before you buy or lease your venue.
- It is helpful to work with a real estate agent, city planner, lawyer, and/or an accountant to get the best deal on a location.

Part 2. Opening Your Car Wash

1. Get the necessary permits and licenses. You will definitely need a permit or a license to open your business. However, the requirements will differ depending on what state you live in. The SBA website maintains a list of business license offices to help you find the information. In addition to a business license, you will need a federal tax identification number and possibly a sales tax license, income tax withholding, and unemployment insurance tax.
- Ask your state business office about the insurance requirements for your car wash business.
- Once you get all of the necessary permits and licenses, keep track of your renewal dates and make a copy for your business records. You will also need to display your license in your car wash so that customers can see it.

2. Buy equipment. The equipment you buy will depend on the type of car wash you have decided to open and the services you offer. Full service car wash, self-service car wash, and an automated car wash will all have different needs.

You will typically need to buy a washing system (e.g. pressure washer, conveyor, self-service equipment, mobile wash systems), chemicals (e.g. cleaning solutions, wax, spot free rinses, protectants, presoaks, etc.), dryers, blowers, vacuums, brushes, towels, compressors, pumps, and a water system (e.g. boilers, water heater, water filtration, extractor, etc.), and billing system.
- Look in trade magazines to buy your chemicals. It is best to buy from big manufacturers.
- Popular equipment manufactures include Ryko, Hannah Industries, Belanger, Karcher, and WashTec.
- Make sure the distributor of your equipment is available to service your equipment when needed. Find out how they handle equipment servicing before you buy from them.

- Equipment typically lasts for 10 years.

3. Market your business. Use a multifaceted approach to advertise your business that includes flyers, posters, and an online presence. The signage for your car wash should be colorful with clear messaging. Make sure that people can easily see it from the road. A popular way to get new customers is by distributing coupons or discounts for car washes. Also, develop relationships with other small businesses located near your car wash.
- Social media is an important aspect of marketing these days. Set up a website and establish a presence on Twitter and Facebook. Make sure any of the paper items that you have include links to your website and social media accounts.
- Use your website to share information about taking care of your car and other relevant tips.
- Schedule a visit to your local radio station to discuss your new business.
- Consider starting a loyalty program. This will encourage repeat customers instead of people who use the coupon one time and never return.

4. Hire employees. A car wash business is very customer-focused. Your employees should be punctual, efficient, skilled, and have excellent communication skills. As you conduct interviews, pay attention to body language and communication skills to get an idea of how the person will interact with customers and coworkers. Always check the references of potential employees as well.

5. Open your car wash. Have a soft opening of your car wash before you have a big grand opening. Wait at least 30 days before you have the big

event. You want to work out some of the kinks and feel comfortable with the car wash before you make a big deal. Think of a grand opening as a party and social event to generate publicity.
- Invite friends, neighboring businesses, your supplies, and the media
- Give away free car washes and promotional items.

Part 3. Running A Profitable Business

1. Add services. Many car washes have combined other services and businesses with their car wash to increase revenue. Additional services will make your car wash more attractive to customers and help your car wash stand out from the crowd. A convenience store restaurant, barber shop, or even an enhanced waiting area (e.g. television, free coffee, comfortable place to sit, etc.) are possible additions. Ask yourself some questions before you invest in an add on service.
- Do I have enough space or will I need additional space?
- How much will it cost?
- What will be the return on my investment?
- Will people buy this service?

2. Offer express detailing services. Express detailing services are services (e.g. wax, sealant, carpet shampoo) that can be done in 30 minutes or less and are done to maintain the appearance of your customer's vehicle. Because you already have the space and equipment, you can offer these services at a lower price than a free-standing detail shop. It is also more convenient for your customers to have their car washed and detailed at one location.
- It is important that you complete the detailing portion of your services quickly. The speed and low cost of the service make it attractive to your customers.

- Make sure that you advertise your detailing services to your customers.
- Check the prices of similar services at a free-standing detail shop to help you determine your prices. Also, check the prices of other car washes in your area that offer these services so that you can be competitive.

3. Use text messages to contact customers. Text marketing is a low cost, effective way to market your business to your customers. Your customers will redeem mobile coupons at a much higher rate than printed coupons. Even if a customer does not use a coupon, you are still building your brand and making your business known.
- Choose a keyword (e.g. water, wash, clean) and advertise by saying, "Text water to 12345 to get special discounts, specials, or coupons." You could also say "Text 12345 to get $3 off your next car wash."
- It only costs one or two pennies to send a text message.
- Text your customers once a month with a special.

4. Offer monthly or unlimited passes. Monthly and unlimited passes offer steady revenue even when customers are not actually coming in for a car wash. This is also a method you can use to build a steady customer base. Carefully price these passes. The price should be low enough so customers feel they are getting a good deal, and high enough for you to make a profit.

Consider pricing your passes to cost of 2 or 3 times the price of a single wash. If you find that customers are not interested, you may need to adjust your price.

You can offer different price points based on the type of car washes you offer. For example, a monthly pass for basic car washes would be less expensive than a monthly pass for premium car washes.

CASHBACK REWARDS CARD

What is cashback?

When you buy something, you get a percentage of the amount it cost paid back to you. This means cashback is a way of getting money off things you buy – think of it as a reward or incentive. It's normally a feature of credit cards, but some current accounts also have cashback. Often cashback is offered on specific purchases, like fuel or for bills. But many providers now offer cashback on anything that you buy.

How does cashback work?

Each time you use the card, you earn a percentage of your spend back in the form of cashback.

For example if your card pays 2% cashback and you spend $100 in a shop, you will earn $2.

This cashback is generally paid annually, though some cards will pay cashback on a monthly basis. Most cashback cards credit the amount you earned onto your statement, reducing your credit card bill. Some cards send the cashback to a bank account so you can spend it, or let you convert it to points or vouchers. Reward points can normally be exchanged at any point once you have enough to qualify for a 'reward'.

Cashback cards come in various forms:

Some will simply pay a flat rate of cashback, no matter how much you spend or where you spend it, others pay tiered rates of cashback depending on how much you spend. For example, 0.5% if you spend less than $6,000 annually, 1% if you spend more than that. Be careful this doesn't tempt you to spend more than you can afford to repay comfortably.

Some cards offer different rates of cashback depending on where you spend your money. For example, 1% on money spent in supermarkets, 2% on money spent in department stores and 3% on money spent on fuel.

When cashback cards are a good idea

If you pay your credit card bill off in full every month then cashback credit cards can be a great idea as you're getting rewarded for spending money that you would have spent anyway. If you don't always pay off your credit card bill in full, then cashback credit cards are not such a good choice.

While you'll earn cashback on your spending, this will usually be less than the interest charged on your outstanding debt.

Don't get taken advantage of

Card providers might attempt to convince you to take out a cashback credit card by coming up with all sorts of scenarios where you'll earn a small fortune in cashback.

For example, they might use your spending on fuel or lunch at work to boost your total spend, and therefore the cashback you could earn, from the card.

However, if you normally pay for these things by debit card or cash, and don't intend to change that behavior, you won't see the benefit in cash back. If you're not comfortable paying by credit card for these things or you worry about getting into debt, you should avoid taking out a card. If you have a cashback card, don't be tempted to spend more just to earn cashback or reward points.

Fees

Another thing to bear in mind before taking out a cashback credit card is that you might have to pay an annual or monthly fee for the card. Factor this fee in. If you only do a little spending on your card each month and don't want to increase that spending, then it might be that any cashback you would have earned will be wiped out by the fee.

Your spending habits

If you want to earn the most cashback possible, it can make sense to put all of the spending you usually do each month onto your credit card. Yet, you shouldn't see this as an excuse to spend more than you usually would, simply to earn more cashback. That extra cashback can be irrelevant if you're unable to pay off the credit card bill each month as it could easily be outweighed by interest charges.

The golden rule of cashback credit cards

Always aim to pay off your credit card each month on time, and in full, otherwise any money earned in cashback will be taken away by interest owed or fees.

CREATE BUSINESS SYSTEM & FRANCHISE IT OUT

American business franchises account for well over $1 trillion in revenue.

American franchises have an enviable rate of success compared to other American businesses. Franchisers provide their franchisees with three advantages that most entrepreneurs do not have: an established business system, a profitable plan and financing. Of these three advantages, the critical differentiator is the established business system, what I call a Business Operating System.

The news and our neighborhoods are filled with stories of companies going out of business or reducing their workforces significantly. However, you might be hard pressed to find a McDonalds, Starbucks, Subway or any other franchise who has closed one of its locations in your neighborhood. So, what can we learn from the successes of the American franchise business?

Business Operating System

A Business Operating System (BOS) is your company's unique way of doing things—how it operates, goes to market, produces and deals with its customers. An effective BOS transcends the people who are doing and managing the work, and is more valuable as a result. A business that effectively operates without you is always more attractive to public and private sources of capital.

In order to create an effective BOS it is key to view your product as the business itself rather than the commodity/service you produce. This paradigm enables the leader to think of the business as a model for 100 others just like it. For example, McDonald's commodity - hamburgers and fries—are not claimed to be the best. However, McDonald's product—its business operating system—is undoubtedly one of the best.

Although many companies spend the time and resources needed to create their BOS, they are disappointed with the results. This is because the components of a BOS are held together by The X Factor.

The X Factor is the same thing that sets great companies apart from their competition. I am frequently asked, "How do Southwest Airlines and The Container Store achieve outstanding results and create such a great place to work?" A closer inspection reveals that their success is less about incredibly innovative management practices and all about The X Factor—discipline.

Great companies create and reinforce a rigorous discipline about the little things that affect their customers, employees and shareholders. They have instilled a discipline in their business (via a BOS) and reinforced discipline at a personal level (via their cultures). Personal and organizational discipline help breathe life into your BOS and enable you to sustain it over time, making it the way you do business rather than just a set of hollow procedures.

Components of Your Business Operating System

It is important to create each BOS component to be scalable, up or down, for future growth or contraction. The components are interrelated as with any living system. Therefore, the successful leaders address all components and understand how they affect each other.

A description of the five components is presented in priority order for effectively creating your BOS.
- Processes
- Systems
- Roles
- Skills
- Structure

1. Processes

Underdeveloped work processes are the most common risk factor for growing companies, and are the first thing that will crater a company in tough economic conditions. In addition to traditional work processes, we include other processes like communication, decision-making and conflict resolution. It is easy to say, "We need a new system".

However, effective leaders have the discipline to resist the illusion that a new system will solve their problems. Streamline your manual processes before changing technical systems. Companies who jump into a new system typically automate their own inefficiencies. This is why Processes should be the first BOS component you create.

Effective processes are:
- Clear
- Replicable
- Documented
- Supported by tools
- Easily accessible.

2. Systems

This component addresses hard and soft systems including: technology, financial, marketing, operations and people. A hard people system is your payroll and human resources information system, whereas soft people systems include performance management, selection, compensation and development systems. Well-designed and applied systems create predictable customer and employee experiences and also enhance your operational efficiency.

Looking at the 80/20 Rule, the 20% of the most effective employees (who produce 80% of the results) inevitably use some kind of a system to enhance their effectiveness. A client recently had to let go of 70% of its sales force and found that the remaining 30% actually accounted for 90% of the company's revenue. Sure enough, the remaining sales people were disciplined in using a system of prospecting, qualifying, proposing, presenting and closing business.

3. Roles

Defining clear roles is a big challenge that requires significant personal discipline. You should write a job description (even if a brief one) for all roles within your desired BOS. Remember to focus on the role itself, not the person.

At the early stages of your BOS, one person may play multiple roles. By creating the roles first, you acknowledge this. As your company changes, predefined roles will enable you to make more effective decisions about which roles an employee should continue or discontinue doing and who you should add/delete from the payroll to effectively implement this change.

Resist jumping to the structure component when defining roles—again this requires personal discipline. This step is about defining the required roles to accomplish your company's mission, not how those roles relate to each other.

4. Skills

Now that you have clear roles that your business requires, you can more precisely match the necessary skills to each role. Effective processes and systems will ensure the highest and best use of your talent. Your systems and processes should be created for the lowest common denominator so they are not people-dependent.

This will free up your employees' minds and time so they can focus on more creative, proactive ways to improve your business. It is common to see talented employees who are underemployed because they are using excess time trying to figure out how to get their work done.

When you fill your roles, it is important to match the role requirements with the employee's skills and natural style. Ensuring a skills match has obvious benefits. Matching the role with the employee's natural style is subtler but is often even more critical. This can be achieved via a simple style assessment and helps the employee be successful.

We all can remember a time when we were in a role for which we were not ideally suited, resulting in greater stress and lower productivity than we (and the company) would prefer.

5. Structure

The key to an effective organizational structure is to design it before you need it—then grow into it. It takes great discipline for leaders to design the other four BOS components before they design their organizational structure. In fact, tinkering with structure is one of the great executive past-times. Unfortunately, this tinkering typically ignores the other, more substantial components.

Structure dictates process. That's why I have outlined the sequence of BOS components in this order. If you create a structure first, your business process will be constrained by your structure and may not reflect the needs of your business and customers. Defining your processes and systems first, as we suggest, results in an organizational structure that supports the way you do business rather than constraining it.

Winston Churchill said, "For the first 25 years of my life I wanted freedom. For the next 25 years I wanted order. For the next 25 years I realized that order is freedom". Your BOS will provide you and your business the order and freedom to work on your business rather than in it.

Although I suggest a particular sequence for creating your BOS, most companies have naturally created one or more of the five components. Since each component may be developed at different levels, it is helpful to prioritize the readiness of each component.

DROPSHIPPING

Drop shipping is an extremely popular business model for new entrepreneurs, especially Millennials, due to internet marketing skills far outweighing financial capacity. Since you don't need to stock or handle the items you are selling, it's possible to start a drop shipping business with limited funds.

A e-commerce website that operates a drop shipping model purchases the items it sells from a third-party supplier or manufacturer, who then fulfills the order. This not only cuts operational costs, but it also frees up your time to focus all of your efforts on customer acquisition.

If you are ready to start a business that can compete with retail giants, and do so on a limited budget, then follow the six steps below. While it doesn't take a lot of startup funds to launch a drop shipping business, it will require an immense amount of hard work.

1. *Select a niche*

The niche you select needs to be laser-focused and something you are genuinely interested in. A product range that isn't focused will be difficult to market. If you aren't passionate about the niche you select, you will be more apt to becoming discouraged, because it takes a lot of work to successfully scale a drop shipping business. Here are some points to consider when selecting your niche:

Seek attractive profits. When you are running a drop shipping business model, your focus is on marketing and customer acquisition, so the amount of work required to sell a $20 item is essentially the same as it would be to sell a $1,500 item. Select a niche with higher-priced products.

Low shipping costs are very important. Even though your supplier or manufacturer will handle the shipping, if the cost is too high, it will act as customer repellant. Find something that is inexpensive to ship, as this also gives you the option of offering free shipping to your customers and absorbing that cost as a business expense in order to attract more sales.

Make sure your product appeals to impulse buyers with disposable income. When you are focused on driving traffic to your website, you want to experience the highest conversion rate possible because most visitors will never return. The products you are selling should trigger impulse buys and appeal to those with the financial ability to make a purchase on the spot.

Make sure people are actively searching for your product. Use Google's Keyword Planner and Trends to check some common search terms related to your potential niche. If nobody is searching for what you are planning on selling, you are dead in the water before you even begin.

Create your own brand. Your drop shipping business will have more value if you can rebrand whatever it is you are selling and pass it off as your own. Look for a product or line you can white label and sell as your own brand with custom packaging and branding.

Sell something that isn't readily available locally. Pick something your customer can't find down the street. That way, you become more attractive to a potential customer.

2. *Perform competition research*

Remember, you will you be competing with other drop shipping operations as well as retail giants like Walmart and Amazon. This is where a lot of potential drop shippers go wrong, because they look for a product that has little to no competition. That's a sign there isn't demand for that particular product.

There are many reasons why a product might not have a lot of competition, like high shipping costs, supplier and manufacturing issues or poor profit margins. Look for products that have competition, as it's a sign that there is a high demand and the business model is sustainable.

3. *Secure a supplier*

Partnering with the wrong supplier can ruin your business, so it's important that you don't rush this step. Conduct proper due diligence. Many drop shipping suppliers are located overseas but I don't recommend using overseas suppliers for many reasons. One reason would be communication due to language barriers. Also, customer wait time to receive the items ordered can be excessive.

Personally, I recommend U.S Dropshipping Suppliers because customers receive their orders in timely manners. For a list of USA Dropshipping suppliers, try reading "Top Sellers Dropshipping Suppliers Revealed!!!"

Try to learn from other entrepreneurs who have walked this path in the past. There are plenty of information sources available, from business and tech blogs to this subreddit about drop shipping. It's a popular topic that can help you avoid costly supplier mistakes.

4. Build your e-commerce website

The fastest way to launch a website that supports a drop shipping business model is to use a simple e-commerce platform like Shopify. You don't need a tech background to get up and running, and it has plenty of apps to help increase sales.

Even if you have a sizeable budget that would allow you to hire a web design and development company to create a custom solution, it's a much wiser move to use one of the plug-and-play options, especially in the beginning. Once you are established and the revenue is coming in, then you can explore additional website customization.

5. Create a customer acquisition plan

Having a great product and a website is great, but without customers looking to buy, you don't have a business. There are several ways to attract potential customers, but the most effective option is to start a Facebook ad campaign.

This allows you to generate sales and revenue right from the start, which can contribute to quick scaling. Facebook allows you to place your offer directly in front of a highly targeted audience. This gives you the ability to compete with the largest brands and retailers immediately.

You also have to think long-term, so search engine optimization and email marketing should also be a focus. Collect emails from the start and set up automated email sequences that offer discounts and special offers. It's an easy way to leverage your existing customer base and generate revenue without additional advertising and marketing spend.

6. Analyze and optimize

You need to track all of the data and metrics available to grow your business. This includes Google Analytics traffic and Facebook conversion pixel data, if that is your main customer acquisition channel. When you are able to track every single conversion — to know where the customer originated from and what path they took on your website that eventually led to a sale — it enables you to scale what works and eliminate what doesn't.

You will never have a set-and-forget advertising or marketing solution. You need to constantly test new opportunities and fine-tune current campaigns, which allows you to know when to optimize or shift campaign spend.

EBATES

The Smart Shopper is a blog from Ebates that helps you save money on everything from home and fashion to electronics and travel. We're all about getting you the biggest bang for your buck with coupons, promo codes and discounts at stores you already know and love. Plus, we'll help you out with tips on stacking your savings with Ebates Cash Back and exclusive deals.

What is Ebates?

Ebates is where you can get Cash Back for shopping at over 2,500 stores. Becoming a member is free! Stores pay Ebates a commission for sending you their way, and Ebates shares the commission with you as Cash Back. Get paid every three months, plus earn a cash bonus when you join and shop. Founded in 1998, Ebates has paid members over $1 billion Cash Back. Start getting yours!

How does Ebates work?

Ebates gets a commission from stores when you make a purchase, and instead of keeping it, Ebates share it with you. Find the store on ebates.com, click "Shop Now" and shop like normal on the store site. After you make an eligible purchase, you'll earn Cash Back and get a check or PayPal payment every quarter.

How to use Ebates:

- Shop with Ebates at your favorite stores
- Earn Cash Back on your orders
- Get paid by check or PayPal — no fees, no forms

How to earn more Cash Back at Ebates:

Ebates Cash Back Button: Never miss out on Cash Back! Get our free browser extension to activate Cash Back directly at store sites. The Cash Back Button even automatically applies the best coupons at checkout. Get it here.

- Ebates App: Shop on the go and earn Cash Back anywhere, anytime. Get the free Ebates App for iPhone, iPad and Android for access to App-exclusive deals!
- In-Store Cash Back: You can shop in stores and earn the Cash Back you love! Browse offers, link them to your credit card and shop like normal.
- Cash Back Credit Card: With the Ebates Cash Back Visa® Credit Card, you can earn an extra 3% Cash Back1 on qualifying purchases through Ebates and 1% Cash Back1 everywhere else Visa credit cards are accepted.
- Refer a Friend: If you love Cash Back, so will your friends! Get cash bonuses for spreading the word about Ebates. The more you refer, the more you earn.
- The Ebates Influencer Program: Join our influencer program and get rewarded for being an Ebates ambassador. Enjoy perks like a flat fee for every qualified referral, invites to exclusive events and more.

Join Ebates: (http://bit.ly/2DLPPsE)

ECOMMERCE

According to the U.S. Small Business Administration, online businesses are growing much faster than traditional brick and mortar stores.

It makes sense.

Local retail shops, DIY craft makers, and even bloggers are starting to sell their merchandise and services online.

What separates the successes from the failures? Among other things, a strategy and an excellent website can greatly contribute to the overall success for business owners. Without these, you may be setting your eCommerce site up for failure by building an eCommerce website that is less than effective. If you want to learn how to create an online store that's successful, our eCommerce website guide is the perfect resource for you.

First things first, you'll need a product to sell before you can start with your eCommerce website building. Once you have your product, you can start creating your online store front and designing your eCommerce website! Click below on any of these subcategories to hop directly to the eCommerce tutorial section you need help with, or simply follow along step-by-step below:

- Create your product.
- Determine pricing for your online store.

- Figure out shipping options.
- Choose your eCommerce platform.
- Pick a domain name and brand.
- Build your eCommerce website.
- Set up your merchant account.
- Add a SSL certificate to your website.
- Start selling online!

1. *Decide on your product.*

If you've been dreaming of setting up an online storefront for a while, then you may well already have a product in mind that you'd like to sell. Whether it's something you make, like handcrafted furniture or handmade soap, or something you've found a source for at wholesale prices so you can sell it off at a profit, every eCommerce store has to start with a product.

Do some research to make sure your product is viable. Is there already a market out there for your product? If there is already an established market, consider whether your product is unique enough to break in. Will you be able to compete on pricing?

Develop a MVP and get started.

2. *Set your pricing.*

Pricing can be one of the hardest aspects to get right when running a new business. If you price too low, you'll lose money or just barely break even – which won't make the time and effort you put into your online store worth it. If you price too high, you won't make enough sales and still risk losing money on the whole endeavor.

To figure out what pricing that makes the sense, you have to first figure out your business' finances. This includes:
- the cost of materials to make your product
- web hosting for your eCommerce site
- taxes
- shipping
- the percentage credit cards or Paypal will skim off the top
- additional marketing and advertising costs

Then figure out how much you want to add on top to pay yourself (and make a profit!).

Pricing pro tip: Before you set your final pricing, research what your competition is charging. You may get to bump your prices up a bit (oh happy day!), or you may have to lower them in order to stay competitive.

3. *Research shipping costs and options.*

If you're selling a physical product, how will you deliver it to customers? Your impulse may be to pass on the full cost of shipping to the client, and many online stores do take this route. However, it's important to note that shipping costs can have a strong psychological impact on consumers, with 44% saying they've abandoned an online purchase due to high shipping and handing costs.

Instead, consider offering one of these alternative shipping methods:
- Offer free shipping, no questions asked
- Offer free shipping and up your product pricing slightly to cover the cost
- Offer free shipping for orders of a certain size
- Offer a flat shipping fee

4. *Choose your eCommerce web hosting.*

When it comes to eCommerce, you have two options: use a marketplace that already exists like Etsy or Amazon, or building an eCommerce website and brand that's all your own. If you want a website and brand that's all your own, many website hosting platforms (including HostGator) make it easy to find compatible eCommerce website hosting options that you can work within the same space you use to work on your website. This way you can direct people to youronlinestore.com. You look like a real, live store!

An eCommerce software like Magento will make it easy for you to list your products, set your price, and add a shopping cart to the website. They take care of ensuring the process is intuitive for both you and your customers, so you can just focus on selling.

5. *Pick a domain name and brand.*

This is the fun part for business owners! Just think, what will customers be telling their friends when they talked about that awesome new product they just bought from _____? Fill in the blank with your brand.

Brainstorm words and phrases that say something about the products you'll be selling, and words and phrases that mean something to you. And be sure to stay away from names that have already been copyrighted by other businesses. Follow these top tips for choosing a domain name for your eCommerce website.

6. *Build your eCommerce website.*

Many hosting platforms can make at least part of this step easier by providing or a merchant site builder you can work from rather than having to build a website from scratch. At this stage, you'll also need to work on writing web copy that describes your wares and helps persuade website visitors to buy.

Once you set up your site, you have to do more than just add your products. In addition to product pages, your eCommerce website development and planning should also include the following pages:
- A home page where you feature weekly deals and sale items
- An about page with a brief description of what you do
- A contact or customer service page so customers can easily reach you
- A blog where you post updates, industry news, and helpful tidbits
- Aside from these pages, you will also have to consider your website's theme, eCommerce plugin options, Google Analytics, and all other practical aspects that will help create your online platform.

7. Set up a merchant account.

Online stores need a way to receive money – specifically, a way to receive credit card payments. A merchant account does the very important job of ensuring you can get paid.

You have options that range from big, familiar brand names like Chase and PayPal, to companies more focused on small businesses like BluePay and PaySimple. You will have to pay a small fee to the company in order to get your money, but the ability to accept the money your customers send will make the fees well worth it.

8. Get your SSL certificate.

When you create your site, be sure to install a SSL certificate. These certificates provide the green lock you see next to URLs when you're shopping online, and they keep your customers' private information safe.

PayPal SSL Certificate

If customers are going to hand you their private payment information (or more accurately, enter it into a form on your website), you need to make sure the sensitive details will stay safe. An SSL certificate for your website encrypts all the sensitive information customers provide so that hackers won't be able to grab that credit card information as it's sent over the web.

9. *Start selling!*

Now it's time to start making money.

Once you launch your online store, you should start thinking about promotion. Content marketing, social media, and paid promotion are all areas worth looking into to start getting people to your website. Check out our post on cheap, easy ways to start marketing your business.

If you're not quite ready to make that level of investment in your online store, start with old-fashioned word of mouth. Talk to your friends about it, mention it to professional acquaintances, and bring it up at any events around town likely to attract the kind of people interested in what you're selling.

Wrapping Up

Brick and mortar business will likely always be around, but the internet gives users access to a larger selection of products and services. Now, the world has access to YOUR products and YOUR services. Once you have learned how to set up an eCommerce website for your eCommerce business, take a moment to pat yourself on the back. You're an entrepreneur now. Then get back to work!

GET PAID TO HAVE AN APP ON YOUR PHONE

The times are tough and almost all of us need a little extra cash in our pockets. Money earning mobile apps are getting popular by the day. Reason being that you can easily make money on the go and aren't limited to your desktop PC anymore.

So here's a comprehensive guide on these top ten apps.

Cash-for-Apps

Cash for Apps is an app that allows its users to earn money by downloading other apps and running them. How it works is that there's a list of available apps to download and each app has different points that are paid for downloading them. You will earn approximately $.10- $.50 per app. Whats good about this app is that its a simple way to make extra money without having to do anything.

How does Cash-for-Apps Pay

This app pays you in points for downloading its apps. Most apps in the list pay from 10-70 points, this can be earned for either running the app or doing a small task on the downloaded app. These points are then redeemed for gift cards or mobile phone recharge.

FeaturePoints App

FeaturePoints app is another application that lets you earn money or redeem gift cards by downloading other apps. It works the same way as Cash-for-Apps does; but if you are looking to get paid in cash for downloading such apps, this is one of the best applications for it.

Once you download the app on your Android/iOS device, go to the store page that shows you a list of apps to download. Here you can earn points for downloading apps from the list, and you use these app for about 2 minutes to earn your points.

How does FeaturePoints Pay

This app pays you though points. You can redeem these points for cash though PayPal, though gift cards or rewards like Amazon gift card, iTunes, Starbucks, etc. The downloadable apps pay you from 50-100 points per download. The user needs to collect 600 points to redeem any reward. Where 600 points equal to $1.

Surveys On The Go

Survey On The Go app is like its name describes it, a survey taking app that pays you in real cash. Here you get paid to take surveys on a variety of topics like entertainment, technology, food, etc. The app works on both Android and iOS devices but its only for the users in the US.

So once you download the app and sign up for it, you have to first do demographic surveys for $.50. These surveys will help the app get more surveys for you in the future. There's also a variety of topics you can choose from in the list. You can even turn on your location to get more targeted surveys. Make sure you keep opening the app to check if surveys are available or not.

How does Survey-On-The-Go Pay

This app pays its users through PayPal. The surveys you take can pay anywhere from $0.25 – $5 each, which is more than any other app will pay you. The minimum payout for this app is $10.

CoSign

CoSign is another great app that lets you earn money by uploading photos on social media. It works by taking pictures of products you like or have and uploading them on on social media platforms like Facebook, Instagram, Pinterest with the description about the product along with its cost. These products can be of any sort, from clothing, to tech products to house hold items, basically just about anything.

After uploading the pictures of these products, you have to tag these products from over 1200 retailers on the CoSign app. This is done by searching for your product by brand name or retailer and drag/drop the correct name on the picture description. So when any of your followers purchase the product displayed, you will earn a commission of 35% of the product price.

How does CoSign Pay

The company pays you through PayPal, Check or gift card. As mentioned before, you earn 35% commission for every product that sells. And you earn points every time anyone views the product or buys it, these points can then be traded for cash. The minimum cash out is $40. So the more products you share the more you'll earn.

Fronto

Fronto is an Andriod lock screen app that pays you to unlock your phone screen and see an ad. Once you download the app, its starts showing you targeted ads on your lock screen. Every time you unlock your phone screen, you interact with the ad and you instantly get paid. How it works is that once you download the app, you fill out your profile along with your interests. The app will then show you ads related to your interests. And every time you unlock your phone, you earn points that can be exchanged for cash.

How does Fronto Pay

Fronto pays its users through PayPal or Amazon Gift card. For every encounter with an ad you earn points. Once you gather enough points, you can exchange them for cash or gift cards.

iPoll

iPoll app pays you to share your opinions about any experiences or products. Basically the app requires you to complete surveys of any kind for market research and pays you cash for your time. There are two types of missions or surveys you can do; one is location based, where you have to go to a specific location/business and complete a survey about your experience. And the second type is to watch a video or complete a survey to earn cash.

How does iPoll Pay

iPoll pays its users through PayPal or Retail Vouchers. The company pays you $5 for signing up with them. And they pay you $0.50 to $3 for every survey you complete. The minimum cash out is $50.

TaskRabbit

TaskRabbit is an app that pays you to perform small tasks for other people. According to your location, the app will show you tasks to perform in your area, you will simply bid on the task you want to perform and complete it to get paid. These tasks can be like picking up grocery, small household repairs, get food and other mundane stuff.

To start on these task, first you have to fill out an application. After that a background check will be conducted and if the company is interested, they will set up a video interview. After that you can begin working as a TaskRabbit tasker.

How does TaskRabbit Pay

The app pays its taskers through PayPal or Check. Although there is no exact amount to performing each task because you have to bid on them and get paid the money to bid on the tasks; there are people who earn $10-$20 per hour performing the tasks. The minimum cash out is $25.

CheckPoints

This app allows you to earn points to check into different stores, watch videos and other stuff. These points can later be redeemed for gift cards. To start making points you have to download the app and get signed up. After that you can make points by going to the "check in" page that displays different stores you are paid to check in at, or watch videos or get paid to sign up on different websites.

How does CheckPoints Pay

CheckPoints app pays though gift cards from stores like Target, Amazon, Walmart etc. You can redeem a $1 gift card for 350 points that you make. You can make 50-100 points watching videos for 3 minutes and 15-25 points for checking in.

Phewtick

Phewtick app that pays you to meet people! You make cash by playing games and redeeming points. How it works is you set up your account on facebook. So once you log in, the app reads your locations and shows you a list of people and their profiles to interact with. The app provides you with a QR code that is to be scanned by the partner to prove they have met. Then you play a game together for points.

How does Phewtick Pay

This app pays you though PayPal or Direct deposit. Where 10 points equal $ .01.

App Trailers

App Trailer is an app that allows you to earn some money by watching videos. If you have some free time on your hands then this app will be great for you. How it works is simple; download the app, login to the system and start watching videos like music, movie or game videos.

You can also earn points by uploading videos and also by getting likes your videos. Once you have accumulated your points, you can redeem them for gift cards or cash.

How does App Trailers Pay

This app pays you either though PayPal or through gift cards from Amazon, itunes, Sephora, Footlocker, etc. Each video length is 30 seconds and you get rewarded 5 points for each video. Where 10 points equal to one cent.

GOOGLE ADSENSE

Google AdSense is a advertising program that allows you to run ads on your website or blog, or YouTube videos, and get paid when when visitors click on them. The ads are generated from businesses that use Google's AdWords program.

For new websites or blogs, the AdSense program can be one of the fastest ways to generate income, which is why it's so popular. But while AdSense is free and easy to use, there are aspects you need to understand about it, and things you can do to maximize your success with it.

Pros and Cons to Making Money with Google AdSense

The Google AdSense program has several great advantages including:
- It's free to join.
- Eligibility requirements are easy, which means you can monetize your website or blog even when it's new.
- There are a variety of ad options and several you can customize to fit the look and feel of your site.
- Google pays monthly (if you meet the $100 threshold) by direct deposit.
- You can run ads on several websites from one AdSense account.
- There are options to run ads on mobile devices and RSS feeds.
- You can easily add it to your YouTube and Blogger accounts.

With that said, there are a few drawbacks to AdSense as well:
- Google can terminate your account in an instant, and it's not very forgiving if you break the rules.
- Like all forms of online income, you need traffic in order to make money.
- When people click on an AdSense ad, you do make some money, but your visitor also leaves your site, which means you lose the opportunity to make money with higher paying affiliate products or your own products and services.
- It doesn't necessarily pay more than other similar programs.

AdSense is a great monetization option, but it's not a get-rich-quick or make-money-doing-nothing program. Further, Google has a lot of rules that aren't always noticed upfront. As a result, many website owners have found out the hard way that they'd violated a Google policy, and have lost their account forever.

Types of AdSense Ads

Google offers a variety of ad types to run on your website, including:

Text: Text ads use words, either as an Ad Unit (one offer) or a Link Unit (list of offers), and come in a variety of sizes. You can customize the color of the box, text and link.

Images: Image ads are graphic ads. They come in a variety of sizes. You can choose an option that mixes both text and image ads.
- Video
- Rich media ads include HTML, Flash or other interactive feature.
- Audio
- AdSense for Search allows you to have a Google search box on your site. When a user enters a term and conducts a search, a search results page opens with AdSense ads. You can customize the color

scheme of the search results page to harmonize with your web site.

Google AdSense Payments

Google pays monthly through direct deposit or check, but will not issue an AdSense payment until your earnings reach or exceed $100. If you don't earn $100 in one month, your earnings roll over and are added to the next month. Each time you reach the $100 threshold, Google will issue a payment on the next payment period. Through your AdSense account, you can see your current earnings, what ads are generating the most clicks, and more.

Making Money with AdSense

Making a significant amount of money with AdSense requires a plan. Here are tips for maximizing AdSense revenue:
- Read and adhere to Google's rules. Webmasters must comply with Google's webmaster policies as well as the AdSense program policy.
- Don't click on your own ads or ask others to click on them. Incentivizing clicks, buying Pay Per Click (PPC) space, or using a program designed to drive traffic to AdSense pages are against the rules. Remember, Google isn't very forgiving about breaking the rules, so be sure to adhere to them.
- Have great content your target market wants to read. Ultimately, money is made, whether through AdSense or other monetization methods, by providing valuable content and quality traffic to your blog or website.
- Use honest, organic traffic building website marketing techniques, especially search engine optimization and article marketing.
- Make sure your website/blog is optimized for mobile (responsive). The number of people who use mobile devices is high. Also make sure you're using responsive ads, so Google can send appropriate ad sizes to mobile devices viewing your site.

- Test ad types and placement to find the options that lead to the most income. Start with standard sizes (300×250, 728×90, and 160×600) as there will more ad options for Google to run.
- Max out your ad placement. You're allowed 3 standard ad placements per page. Use them all for maximum benefit.
- Have ads above the fold (the part of your page first seen without scrolling).
- Have a leader board ad below your header/logo instead of at the very top of the page, where it's more likely to be noticed.
- Include in-content ads for viability.
- Monitor your results. Google can overwhelm you with tools and feedback, but do your best to check out what it says about your results so you can make the most of your effort.

Read email from Google, especially if it's sending a warning about something it doesn't like on your site. Failure to deal with Google's complaints will lead to termination of the program.

Advanced AdSense Tips

Once you have ads running on your site, you'll want to make sure you getting the most of your AdSense program. Here are some additional tips to consider when you're ready to boost your AdSense income:

Run Experiments - You can A/B test your ads through AdSense.

Experiment with link and box colors - If you're colors match your theme, consider changing them up to see if it impacts results.

Enable placement targeting - This allows advertisers to choose where their ads appear. Set up custom channels so you can get a better sense of what's working and not working

Dealing with Competitors' or Questionable Advertisements

If you offer products or services on your website, you may find that some ads Google delivers come from your competitors. Another issue that can occur is ads that may not be completely legitimate or they might offend your market. To prevent these offers from showing up on your site, Google AdSense allows you to block up to 200 URLs from appearing on your site.

The challenge of this is two-fold.

You don't know what ads are running on your site until you see them there. Plus, with each page load, and depending on the visitors browsing history, the ad may not show up again or it might appear in a different spot.

Since you can't click on your own links (to the get the URL), you need to be careful about obtaining the URL to block. The best way to get the link so you can block it in AdSense is to right click the link, select "Copy Link Address," and paste it into a document or text editor (i.e. Notepad). The Google URL is really long, but you're looking for the section that identifies the advertiser. Copy that link, and paste into your AdSense blocked ads account.

Other Programs Besides AdSense

There are many ad network programs similar to AdSense, such as Media.net and InfoLinks. Some might require a traffic threshold, so you'd need to wait until your site is established before being accepted. Most have similar rules to Google, such as a limit to the number of the network's ads per page (usually 3) and termination for clicking your own ads. In most cases, you can run different ad networks on your site without violating terms of service, but you'll want to read the rules of each network before doing it.

Further, you want to avoid your site becoming so overwhelmed with ads that your readers can't find the content.

Other Income Options besides Ad Networks

Ad networks, especially AdSense, are great options because you can join as a new blogger or website owner, and are easy to use. But they're not the only ways to make money from your website. In fact, as your site traffic grows, other monetization options might be better. Here are some other money-making ideas you can use instead of, or along with, ad networks.

Affiliate Marketing: Like ad networks, affiliate programs are usually free to join and easy to add to your website.

Sell Your Own Product or Service: When you have a readership and social media following, you have an audience that trusts and likes you. As a result, they're more open to buying directly from you. Creating your own product or service, as opposed to promoting someone else through affiliate marketing, can earn you significantly more money. This is especially true with information products or online courses that are inexpensive to create and sell. Other options include ebooks and freelance services.

Coaching or Consulting: As an expert in your topic, you're in a good position to help people beyond the information you provide on your website/blog, to offer more in depth help through coaching or consulting.

Sponsors: When you have a good amount of traffic and terrific influence over your audience, other companies will pay to sponsor your website. They can sponsor your entire site, which would cost them more, or a single page. Some just have advertising.

As you can see, there are many ways to earn income from a website or blog. But many require that you have traffic and an audience that is paying attention to you before they make any money. This is where AdSense is a good beginning monetization option. You don't have to create anything, it's free to join, and it's easy to add the ad code to your website.

Join Google Adsense: (http://bit.ly/2Inn3V7)

LAUNDROMAT

Laundromats make it easier to get laundry done when customers either don't have a washing machine at home or need to wash more clothing than their machines can handle at home. Laundromats also sell detergents and soaps, dryer sheets, and other related items to help customers get their laundry done.

Who is this business right for?

This business is good for people who are looking for a full-time business but who also want something they can start in their spare time. Running a laundromat can either be a very hands-on or more passive business, allowing the entrepreneur to have flexible hours and scheduling. However, as this business grows, it requires a great deal of management. Unless you can afford to hire a manager, this is a time-consuming business to own long-term.

What happens during a typical day at a laundromat?

Running a laundromat can be simple or more involved. It all depends on the type of laundromat you want to run. A simple business model for this type of business is an unmanned laundromat service. A more involved version of this business would include daily monitoring of the laundromat, collecting money from customers, folding clothes for those who paid for full service, and managing the books.

What is the target market?

Preferred clients are businesses with long-term service contracts. However, a laundromat can also service the general public and bring in a consistent stream of revenue. Ideal customers are those living in apartments where there are no onsite laundry services or washers and dryers for self-service. This might mean placing the laundromat near low-rent or poor neighborhoods.

How does a laundromat make money?

A laundromat makes money by charging customers to wash and dry their clothes. A laundromat may choose to operate as a self-serve operation, where customers insert quarters into machines to operate the washers and dryers, or it may be run as a full-service business in which customers pay to have staff do their laundry for them.

This business usually handles transactions in cash. However, some laundromats do offer the use of credit cards, checks, and even laundromat-specific cards. Cash-based transactions help to keep costs down for the customers and owner because there are no credit card fees. However, accepting credit cards increases convenience, potentially leading to more customers.

What is the growth potential for a laundromat?

Growth potential for this type of business is almost unlimited. Laundromats can be operated at a small scale, with a single building servicing many customers with a handful of machines. You can even start a small business out of your home, offering full-service laundry and folding services.

It can also be operated at scale with multiple locations across a town or city. Some laundromats operate near colleges and dorms where college students can easily access the building to wash their clothes.

What are some skills and experiences that will help you build a successful laundromat?

Aside from having good business sense, good negotiation skills, and being mechanically-inclined, there are no special skills or education needed to start a laundromat.

What are the costs involved in opening a laundromat?

Costs for starting a laundromat are significant. Depending on the location, it can cost you between $100,000 and $200,000 to buy an existing business or it can cost up to $1 million or more. Businesses you buy in larger cities tend to cost more.

Also, some states are inherently more expensive than others. For example, buying a laundromat in California, Florida, or New York may be much more expensive than buying one in Idaho or Alabama.

If you're starting out of your home, you can start with little to no money upfront. Expect total startup expenses for a small business outside the home to be between $100,000 and $250,000.

A big part of the startup cost is the machines. Get "like new" machines that have been well-serviced and you can save yourself some money and lower your startup costs. However, be aware that used machines may not come with reliable or accurate service records. New machines may initially cost more, but you will also know the entire service history.

If you finance the business, rather than pay cash, you may only need to put down 10% to 30% of the total cost. Utility costs are a big expense.

While the machines themselves can cost you $500 to $700 each for top loader and $3,500 and $20,000 for front loaders, utilities to run them (water, heating, etc.) can run between $200 and $2,000 per month, each.

What are the steps to start a laundromat?

Once you're ready to start your laundromat, follow these steps to ensure that your business is legally compliant and avoid wasting time and money as your business grows:

- Plan your business. A clear plan is essential for success as an entrepreneur. A few important topics to consider are your initial costs, your target market, and how long it will take you to break even.
- Form a legal entity. Establishing a legal business entity prevents you from being personally liable if your laundromat is sued.
- Register for taxes. You will need to register for a variety of state and federal taxes before you can open for business.
- Open a business bank account. A dedicated checking account for your laundromat keeps your finances organized and makes your business appear more professional to your customers.
- Set up business accounting. Recording your various expenses and sources of income is critical to understanding the financial performance of your business. Keeping accurate and detailed accounts also greatly simplifies your annual tax filing.
- Obtain necessary permits and licenses. Failure to acquire necessary permits and licenses can result in hefty fines, or even cause your business to be shut down.
- Get business insurance. Insurance is highly recommended for all business owners. If you hire employees, workers compensation insurance may be a legal requirement in your state.
- Define your brand. Your brand is what your company stands for, as well as how your business is perceived by the public. A strong

brand will help your business stand out from competitors.
- Establish a web presence. A business website allows customers to learn more about your company and the products or services you offer. You can also use social media to attract new clients or customers.

Should you consider joining a franchise?

Joining a laundromat franchise can be a good option for entrepreneurs who prefer to use a proven model rather than start from scratch. While joining one can mean slightly higher initial costs and less control, a quality franchise offers great benefits such as initial and ongoing support, marketing assistance, and brand recognition. Opening a laundromat franchise typically requires $230,000-$600,000.

What are some insider tips for jump starting a laundromat?

These businesses sink or swim based on location. Try to get good real estate for your laundromat. Usually, this means setting up shop in neighborhoods where local residents don't have easy access to laundry services and machines. Another tip is to focus on securing a few small corporate clients, like janitorial businesses and restaurants, as clients. This will give you a strong base of income to work off from.

How to promote & market a laundromat

Promoting a laundromat is pretty straightforward. Advertise in local neighborhoods and spread your marketing to areas in your town or city where there is limited access to machines and other laundry services.

How to keep customers coming back

The best laundromats are ones that maintain a clean and friendly environment. When the inside of the building is clean and well-maintained, and when all machines are functioning normally, then customers are more likely to clean up after themselves and treat the machines as their own.

How and when to build a team

A coin laundromat doesn't need a large staff and might be able to be non-staffed. However, you should consider hiring at least one to two employees to watch over the place, encourage customers to pick up after themselves, and to keep the place clean. Each location can be minimally staffed, however.

How much can you charge customers?

Costs for laundry services are driven almost entirely by the location. In bigger cities, you can charge more. In smaller towns, less. On average, you can charge customers $3 per load of laundry, washed and dried.

What are the ongoing expenses for a laundromat?

The biggest ongoing expenses are the utilities. Expect to pay between $200 and $2,000 per machine just for the water and heating. You should also set aside money for maintenance. Maintenance costs can range from $50 to $150 per machine for simple maintenance and repairs.

How much profit can a laundromat make?

The average annual income of a laundromat in the U.S. ranges from $30,000 to $1 million, according to Brian Wallace of the Coin Laundry Association. Average profit margin is between 20% and 30%. Some laundromats make significantly less, however. An owner-operated laundromat may be able to sustain a high profit margin by doing his own maintenance, and working in the business instead of paying an employee. A larger business, with multiple locations, may only net a 10% to 20% margin after operating costs.

How can you make your business more profitable?

One of the best ways to make your business more profitable is to offer additional services. For example, you could offer self-serve dry clean machines, sell detergent, snacks, and coat hangers, dry cleaning bags, and laundry bags. Offer free or discounted wifi Internet services for customers to help them pass the time while they wait for their laundry.

Another way to dramatically reduce costs is to operate your business in an area where taxes and utilities are lower. Check county taxes and water utility rates. These can vary significantly from one location to the next.

Do your own maintenance. Maintenance on washing machines and dryers isn't too difficult for someone with basic handyman skills. If you purchase washers and dryers that are easily serviceable, you can save yourself several thousand dollars per year.

ONLINE ARBITRAGE

Online arbitrage (sometimes referred to as retail arbitrage) is, like all sales ventures, based on the concept, "buy low and sell high," but in this case, it's "buy lower and sell higher." You buy goods online at a lower price than they're currently selling for on Amazon, and then resell them on Amazon at a profit, taking advantage of that price mismatch.

Unlike some other forms of arbitrage or reselling, in online arbitrage you buy online only, not from brick and mortar stores. And you do so as a consumer, at retail prices, not as a business buying at wholesale prices directly from a manufacturer or distributor.

Online arbitrage is not the same as Amazon-to-eBay Arbitrage, which involves finding items available from Amazon and listing them for sale at a higher price on eBay but not actually buying them until the items you've listed sell on eBay.

In online arbitrage as discussed here, the arbitrager buys merchandise before listing it for sale. You can limit your online selling activities to Amazon, or use online arbitrage in addition to selling through another channel, such as your own website or a Shopify store.

In order to list items for sale on Amazon, you'll need to set up a seller account. There is an Individual seller option, but most people who are serious about giving online arbitrage a try will establish a Professional

Seller account. You'll need to familiarize yourself with Amazon's rules for selling. You don't want to find that your account is suspended over an infraction of a rule you weren't even aware of.

Here are some ideas that should help you get started on the path to success in online arbitrage.
- What to Buy
- Where to Buy
- How Much to Pay
- Automated Tools
- Fulfilment by Amazon (FBA)
- Keep It Legal
- It's a Home-Based Business
- Use Social Media
- Invest in Your Success
- Start Small

1. *What to Buy*

Aside from price, which we'll look at shortly, the most important consideration in selecting products to buy for resale is that you want to sell them off quickly, not stockpile them long-term in your garage or basement. Two indicators of a product that will sell well are decent product reviews and a good Amazon seller ranking.

Since you will be taking delivery of the goods you buy, you will need to consider your storage capacity as well. If your only storage space is a hall closet in your home, you probably shouldn't be looking to buy and resell pianos or big-screen televisions. Buying smaller items will also help keep your shipping costs down.

Some online arbitragers leverage their knowledge of a particular niche, such as toys or consumer electronics, or high-end cookware, to develop a specialized business. Others prefer to remain flexible and buy an eclectic assortment of merchandise.

2. *Where to Buy*

In online arbitrage, you buy from online retailers that are known for their low prices and frequent promotions and clearances. In the United States, Walmart.com is a prime example. However, that means that plenty of other online arbitragers will be looking for bargains there, too. You may be better off searching in niche stores, especially if you are specializing in a particular product niche.

3. *How Much to Pay*

Online arbitragers typically look for items selling at no more than half of their current Amazon listing price. The price difference needs to be large enough to cover shipping charges and your listing fees and still leave you with a good profit margin. Bear in mind that prices can change unexpectedly, turning what looked like a profitable deal into a losing proposition.

4. *Automated Tools*

Finding arbitrage opportunities could easily eat up every waking hour if you let it. There is simply no way for one person to monitor enough products and enough sources without using some of the many available automated tools designed specifically to support online arbitrage.

Amazon's price tracking software gives you the price history of all of the products sold on Amazon. Amazon price trackers make it easy to distinguish temporary price anomalies from the typical price for a product over time, helping you avoid acting on a short-term price increase that may well disappear by the time you have purchased units to list for resale.

Amazon also offers revenue calculators to help you determine how much you need to charge for an item to cover fees and make a profit. There are separate revenue calculators for North America (US, Mexico, Canada) and Europe.

There are a number of price monitoring tools that yield daily lists of products you may want to consider buying for resale on Amazon. The Web Retailer Directory is a good source of information about arbitrage deal finders. Most of these tools are available for a monthly fee (typically from $20 to $100 per month).

5. *Fulfilment by Amazon (FBA)*

When you use Amazon's FBA program, you take delivery of the items you have bought for resale, label and package them, box them all up, and ship them to Amazon's warehouse. From that point on, Amazon takes over, assuming responsibility for fulfilling customer orders and providing after-sale customer service. You'll pay the FBS fee, but in the long run, it can save you a lot of time and money that would otherwise go to packaging and shipping each individual customer order. It also means you get to use your hall closet for its intended purpose: storing coats and umbrellas, not merchandise waiting to be sold.

6. *Keep It Legal*

Some online arbitragers have received "cease and desist" letters from the manufacturers of goods they are reselling on Amazon, raising questions as to the legality of online arbitrage. Rest assured that the practice is legal, based on the legal concept of the "first sale." The first sale doctrine establishes the legality of reselling any authentic item that you have obtained through legal means, the word "authentic" being very significant.

You could find yourself in hot water if you sell counterfeit items even if you buy them from established retailers, believing them to be authentic. If the manufacturer becomes aware that you are selling counterfeits, you could be sued for trademark infringement.

The simple solution is to avoid buying designer products that carry major, well-known labels, because those manufacturers keep a close eye on Amazon, eBay, Etsy and other online sellers to try to maintain control over their valuable trademarks and avoid dilution of their brands.

Even so, manufacturers of trademarked goods often distribute their products only through authorized sellers, and if you don't have a distributorship agreement with them, you might receive one of those "cease and desist" letters.

7. It's a Home-Based Business

Another aspect of keeping it legal is to run your online arbitrage operation as a legitimate home-based business. Set up a legal business entity, whether it's a sole proprietorship, a limited liability corporation (LLC), or something else. Get some legal and tax advice to make sure that you're in compliance with applicable local, state, and federal laws and regulations.

Keeping detailed records of your income and expenses will facilitate the preparation of tax returns and give you a realistic picture of your cash flow and the profitability of your online arbitrage activities. Consider using off-the-shelf accounting software to automate your bookkeeping, check writing, and tax preparation.

8. *Use Social Media*

Successful online arbitragers typically use social media to drive traffic to their Amazon listings, so try to learn something about social media marketing if the concept is new to you. Try embedding a link to your Amazon page in your posts on Facebook, Instagram, Twitter, and any other social media platform you use.

Getting your social media followers to Amazon, which has a higher conversion rate than any other website, should boost your sales significantly, especially if your followers share your posts with others. Try setting up a business page on Facebook and using Facebook ads to direct visitors to your Amazon page.

9. Invest in Your Success

Invest the time to learn more about online arbitrage before diving into it headfirst. There are numerous online resources, from blogs to YouTube videos, to full-blown courses that will help you educate yourself. Decide how much money and time you're able to put into launching your arbitrage business. Be prepared to spend at least a few hundred dollars to get started.

Learn as much as you can about all of the fees and expenses you'll incur so that you can set your pricing to yield a reasonable profit. And understand that online arbitrage involves some degree of risk, most notably the risk that the price mismatch could disappear before you sell out your inventory of an item.

10. *Start Small*

Try wading before you venture into the deep end of the pool. Once you have a firm grasp of the process, try it out with a few select items, or even a relatively small quantity of one item, to test out your assumptions about demand and pricing. Many online arbitragers work at it for only a few hours a week, regarding it as an additional income stream rather than a primary source of income. Others eventually become full-time arbitragers, but the majority fall somewhere in between. You'll find the involvement level that suits you best once you've gained some experience in online arbitrage.

RESELL ON EBAY

Check your favorite eBay category and see what the hot-selling item is. Better yet, go to your favorite store and make friends with the manager. After you're armed with the information you need, search out that item for the lowest price you can, and then give it a shot on eBay.

Keep these shopping locales in mind when you go on the eBay hunt:

Upscale department stores, trendy boutiques, outlet stores, or flagship designer stores are good places to do some market research. Check out the newest items and then head to the clearance area or outlet store and scrutinize the bargain racks for brand-name items.

Discount club stores such as Sam's Club and Costco made their mark by selling items in bulk to large families, clubs, and small businesses. In case you haven't noticed, these stores have upscaled and sell just about anything you could want.

Dollar stores in your area. Many of the items these places carry are overruns (too many of something that didn't sell), small runs (too little of something that the big guys weren't interested in stocking), or out-of-date fad items that need a good home on eBay.

Garage, tag, moving, and estate sales offer some of the biggest bargains you'll ever come across. The stuff you find at estate sales is often of a higher quality. Keep an eye out for "moving to a smaller house" sales. These are usually people who have raised children, accumulated a houseful of stuff, and want to shed it so that they can move to a condo in Palm Springs.

Liquidation and estate auctions are two types of auctions where you can pick up bargains. Before you go, double-check payment terms and find out whether you must bring cash or can pay by credit card. Also, before you bid on anything, find out the hammer fee, or buyer's premium. These fees are a percentage added to the winner's bid; the buyer has the responsibility for paying these fees.

When a company gets into serious financial trouble, its debtors obtain a court order to liquidate the company to pay the bills. The liquidated company then sells its stock, fixtures, and even real estate in a liquidation auction. Items sell for just cents on the dollar, and you can easily resell many of these items on eBay.

Estate auctions are the higher level of estate garage sales. Here you can find fine art, antiques, paper ephemera, rare books, and collectibles of all kinds. These auctions are attended mostly by dealers, who know the local going prices for the items they bid on. But because they're buying to sell in a retail environment, their high bids will generally be the wholesale price for your area.

Newspaper auction listings are an excellent source of merchandise for resale, particularly the listings of liquidations and estate auctions and the daily classified section, which often has ads that announce local business liquidations. Liquidation and estate sales are professionally run, usually by licensed liquidators or auctioneers, and involve merchandise that may be new but is always sold in lots.

Going-out-of-business sales, some of which run week by week, with bigger discounts as time goes by. Don't be shy about making an offer on a quantity of items.

Flea markets or swap meets in your area may have some bargains you can take advantage of.

Gift shops at museums, monuments, national parks, and theme parks can provide eBay inventory — but think about where to sell the items. Part of your selling success on eBay is access. People who can't get to Graceland may pay handsomely for an Elvis mini-guitar with the official logo on the box.

Freebies are usually samples or promotion pieces that companies give away to introduce a new product, service, or, best of all, a media event. Hang on to these! If you receive handouts from a sporting event, premiere, or historic event — or even a collectible freebie from a fast-food restaurant — they could be your ticket to some eBay sales.

For example, when Return of the Jedi was re-released in 1997, the first 100 people to enter each theater got a Special Edition Luke Skywalker figure. These figures are still highly prized by collectors and when the next part of the Star Wars saga was released, the prices on this figure went up yet again.

Design T-Shirts, Mugs and Sell via online marketplaces like Zazzle or Cafepress

Design t-shirts to sell online - 8 companies that pay!Have you ever read a funny slogan or an inspirational quote and thought, "I wish I had a T-shirt that said that!"? I would say most of us (including myself) have. As you might have guessed, this post is going to highlight several sites that pay you to design T-shirts. So if you're someone who is forever having creative flashes and you also happen to be a fairly decent designer, there's potential for you to earn money here!

Today I did lots of digging around and found quite a few sites you can use to get paid to design T-shirts. I want to say upfront that most of these only offer a chance to get paid — you'll have to have a "winning" design, or your shirt will have to receive enough interest from potential buyers. Even so, it may be fun to try out if you think you'd be good at it.

Ways to Design T Shirts to Sell Online

Teespring

Use their easy online designer to create a T-shirt. Set your price, a goal, and then if you collect enough pre-orders, they will manufacture and ship the T-shirt to buyers. One of the best things about this site is that you keep ALL of the profit on T-shirt sales. However, there is of course a chance you won't get enough pre-orders for Teespring to decide to print and ship the shirt. This site is open internationally, although you do have to have a Paypal account for collecting payments if your shirt is sold.

So do people actually make money on Teespring? Looks like it!

SellMyTees

This is another website that will provide you with an online shop for selling your designs on T-shirts. Note that while they do have a free plan for sellers which lets you open up a small basic shop with 20 designs, they do offer paid (monthly) plans as well. SellMyTees pays monthly via Paypal or check, your choice. There is more info on how payment works here.

Threadless

This is an online T-shirt shop featuring designs from many independent artists around the world. Threadless has an ongoing design challenge that you can submit your own designs to.

Members of the Threadless community are allowed to score the designs submitted, and if yours is one of the best of the best, it will be manufactured and sold. You'll get not only a cash prize for having your design selected, but you will also receive ongoing royalties from sales of your design.

In addition, you can set up your own artist shop on Threadless.

Spreadshirt

Spreadshirt allows you to create your own T-shirt designs, upload them, and sell them (pending approval from Spreadshirt). You can also open your own shop on Spreadshirt and sell lots of different designs. According to Spreadshirt, if you sell a $20 T-shirt, you'll get to keep $12 for yourself. They do not charge any fees.

Payments are made quarterly via either bank transfer or Paypal as long as you have $25 in commissions pending. If you have more than $100 pending, you can request a payment monthly.

SpreadShop

This site makes it possible for you to open your very own T-shirt store. Plus there are no fees — the site is completely free for you to use. There are two ways to earn here — by being a marketplace designer and setting your own prices based on what you think your designs are worth, or you can become a shop owner and earn an commission off each sale of your products.

TeePublic

Create your own design for a T-shirt, upload it, and it immediately will go up for sale. For 72 hours, the shirt you design will be priced at just $14 but will go up after that so they encourage promoting it heavily during the first three days. You can check out their commission rates here.

Zazzle

You've probably heard of Zazzle — it's very well-known. You can put your artwork not only on T-shirts, but also on coffee mugs, calendars, posters, and more. Zazzle allows you to open your own online store and also set your own royalty rates for your creations.

CafePress

This is another site very similar to Zazzle and about as equally popular. With CafePress, you can create designs and put them on T-shirts, posters, coffee mugs, etc. and then sell them. You can get your own online branded shop through CafePress. They will handle marketing for your shop and then you can earn royalties on all sales.

START A BLOG OR BUY A BLOG

Here is how to make money from a blog:
- Set up your blog
- Start creating useful content
- Get off your blog and start finding readers
- Build engagement with the readers that come
- Start making money from the readership you have through one or more of a variety of income streams

Sounds easy doesn't it! On some levels the process is simple – but you need to know up front that there's a lot to each step and below I'm going to give you some pointers on each including some further reading.

Here's how to make money from a blog.

1. *Start a Blog*

In order to make money blogging you're going to need to have a blog. While this is pretty obvious it is also a stumbling block for many PreBloggers who come to the idea of blogging with little or no technical background. If that's you – don't worry! It was my story too and most bloggers start out feeling a little overwhelmed by the process of starting their blog.

2. Start Creating Useful Content

A blog is not a blog without content so once you've set your blog up you need to focus your attention upon creating useful content. What you choose to create will depend a little on the topic that you choose to write about (on that note, most successful bloggers have some focus to their blogging whether that be a niche or a demographic that they write for).

The key with creating content is to make it as useful as possible. Focus upon creating content that changes people's lives in some way will be the type of content that people will value the most and it will help people to feel like they know, like and trust you – which is really important if you later want to make money from your blog.

3. Get off your blog and start finding readers

As you create the most useful content that you possibly can it is easy to get very insular with your focus and spend most of your time looking at building your blog. Many bloggers have a 'build it and they will come mentality' with their blogging but this is a bit of a trap. If you want to make money from your blog you need to not only focus upon building a great blog but it is also necessary to get off your blog and to start promoting it.

There are many ways to experiment with growing your blog's audience that I've written in previous blog posts and talked about in podcasts (I'll share some further reading and listening below) but it is important to enter into all these strategies remembering that you should not just be looking for 'traffic' but 'readers'. Start by thinking carefully about the type of reader you'd like to have read your blog.

Once you know who you're hoping to have read your blog ask yourself where that type of person might already be gathering online. Begin to list where they might be gathering:

- Are they reading certain blogs? List the top 3
- Are they participating in certain forums? List the top 3
- Are they listening to podcasts? List the top 3
- Are they engaging on certain social networks? List the top 3
- Which accounts are they following on each of these social networks? List the top 3

Each of these places that you reader might already be gathering has opportunities to develop a presence whether that be by leaving good comments, offering to create guest posts or simply by being helpful and answering questions.

With this list of blogs, focus, podcasts, social media accounts in hand you will have some good spots to begin to hang out and create value. The key is to build a presence, to add value, to foster relationships – not to engage in spammy practices.

4. Build engagement with the readers that come

With sustained focus upon creating great content and finding readers for your blog you'll begin to notice people visiting your blog and engaging with your content. At this point you need to switch your focus to engaging with those readers and building community.

Respond to comments, reach out to those readers personally and do everything that you can to keep them coming back again and again by building a 'sticky blog'. Look after the readers you already have well and you'll find they spread the word of your blog for you and help make your blog even more widely read. Having an engaged reader is also much easier to make money from.

5. *Start making money from the readership you have through one or more of a variety of income streams*

OK – the first four steps of starting a blog, creating content, finding readers and building engagement with those readers are important foundations that you really do need to get in place before you'll be able to build long term income for your blog. There's no avoiding that what we've covered is a lot of work but if you do it well you'll be setting yourself up well and giving yourself every chance of being able to make money from your blog.

With these foundations in place you're now ready to start attempting to make money from your blog but you do need to be aware that just because you have set up your blog, have content and have engaged readers that the money won't just automatically flow.

It takes continued work and experimentation to make money from your blog.

I've written many articles here on ProBlogger on the topic of making money blogging and will link to some suggested further reading on the topic below but let me share a few introductory words on the topic first.

There are Many Ways to Make Money Blogging

One of the biggest misconceptions that I see bloggers having about monetising blogs is that they have to do it in one of a handful of ways. The reality is that there are many ways to make money from blogs.

1. *Advertising Income*

This is where many bloggers start. In many ways this model of making money from blogs is not dissimilar to how a magazine or newspaper sells ads. As your traffic and brand grows you'll find advertisers will be willing to pay to get exposure to your audience. While you need decent traffic to do a direct deal with an advertisers there are ad networks (like Google AdSense) that act as a middleman and enable smaller publishers to run ads on their blogs. This is where many bloggers start (I did too).

2. *Affiliate Income*

A recent survey of ProBlogger readers found that affiliate promotions was the most common type of income that our readers have. To put it most simply – affiliate income is when you link to a product that is for sale on another site (take Amazon for example) and if someone follows your link and ends up buying that product you earn a commission on that sale. There's more to it than that but this is another great place to start with monetising your blog as affiliate programs are easy to sign up for and if you have an engaged audience you will find they follow the recommendations that you make on products.

3. *Events*

While not something most bloggers do I have noticed an increase in the number of bloggers making money by running events. Alternatively online events or summits are getting more popular.

4. *Recurring Income*

Another growing category of income that I'm seeing more and more bloggers are experimenting is recurring income streams (sometimes called continuity programs or membership programs). This is where readers pay a regular recurring amount (usually on a monthly or annual basis) for access to either premium content, a community area, some kind of service, tools, coaching (or some combination of these things).

5. *Promoting a Business*

Many brick and mortar businesses indirectly make money from their blogs by using their blogs to grow their profile and direct readers to their business.

6. *Services*

A common way that many bloggers make money is through offering services to their readers. These might be anything from coaching and consulting, to writing or copywriting, to design, training or other freelance services.

7. *Products*

While I started out making money from my blogs through advertising and affiliate promotions today my #1 source of income is through selling eBooks and courses on my blogs. These 'virtual products' take work to create but have been lucrative for me and many other bloggers.

Products can of course take many forms and income virtual information products like eBooks or courses but also other virtual products like software, reports etc. The other type of product some bloggers sell is physical products. This is most common when the blogger has a business but sometimes bloggers also create merchandise (T-shirts etc) or other physical products to sell.

Other Income Streams

There are of course other forms of income that bloggers experiment with. Some include asking for donations, syndicating content to other sites and lastly selling their blogs.

Multiple Income Streams

Most full time bloggers make money more than one way and end up with multiple income streams. Diversifying your income in this way not only is smart and helps you spread the risk from having all your eggs in one basket but it also speeds up the journey to going full time.

STORAGE RENTALS

There is a ton of bad information out there on the self-storage or mini-storage industry. Contrary to what you may read, there is virtually no money in building new facilities or buying them at a 7% cap rate.

If you really want to make money in self-storage, you have to put in significantly more work, and follow a different game plan entirely. Buying an established facility with good occupancy at market rents will not lead to great riches ' only endless concern over making the note payment. The way to success is much more basic.

Buy low and sell high

Few people make a fortune owning self-storage facilities. They make their money selling them. To make money buying and selling self-storage facilities, you have to understand how to buy at the cheapest possible price and how to sell at the highest possible one. And it's not a whole lot different than other forms of commercial real estate. But it's shrouded in more bad information than most.

A lot of people got spoiled

During the 1970s and 1980s and even 1990s, you could not build a self-storage facility and go wrong. The industry was in its infancy, and the demand outstripped the supply in almost every market in the U.S. As a result, the 'build it and they will come' approach seemed to be 100% accurate at all times. Financing to build was easy to attain, and the facilities just started popping up everywhere ' in big cities and rural markets alike.

The reality of today

Supply and demand have now met, although in some markets supply still overshadows demand. Gone are the days of success being rewarded on poor strategy or execution. Some markets have significant vacancy and rents are stagnant. The good news is that the buildings are easy to maintain and the business model is simple and easy to understand. Plus, the typical customer is relatively stable and seems happy with the relationship.

How to buy them cheap

You need to buy self-storage facilities that are either poorly managed or in distress, such as foreclosure. A stabilized property that is professionally managed has no upside. You want a property where you can increase revenue through higher rents and increased occupancy, and decrease costs through renegotiating all the bills and proactively finding ways to cut costs.

The good news is that there has never been a better time to buy these facilities, as the current economic depression, coupled with the collapse of real estate financing has made these opportunities more abundant.

How to sell them high

Selling a self-storage facility at a good price is made possible today through the internet. Sites such as selfstorages.com and Loopnet.com have opened up the sea of investors to this asset class in a big way. You can reach one hundred times more buyers through internet postings in one month than in an entire career before. Sales is a volume business, and the volume is on your side.

Of course, to get a property sold, it must be reasonably priced. That's why it's essential that you buy them really, really cheap on the front end.

Conclusion

You can make big money in self-storage, but only it you are a very smart buyer and seller. People who pursue average deals will only, best case, achieve average returns, which are less than spectacular. You must seek out deals that are dramatically underpriced and turn them around if you want to really take advantage of this niche.

TAX LIEN CERTIFICATES

A tax lien certificate is a certificate of claim against a property that has a lien placed upon it as a result of unpaid property taxes. Tax lien certificates are generally sold to investors through an auction process.

BREAKING DOWN Tax Lien Certificates

A tax lien certificate is a lien placed on your property for not paying your taxes. Every time your property taxes come due, the municipality will issue a tax lien. When you pay your taxes on time, the lien is removed. If you don't pay your taxes — or don't pay them on time — the town or county will auction off the tax lien certificate to an investor(s). That investor will then pay the taxes on behalf of the property tax owner.

How Tax Lien Certificates Are Sold

Most tax lien sales auctions are conducted by the county or municipality where the property is located. For a property to be eligible, it must be considered tax-defaulted for a minimum period of time depending on local regulation. Instead of bidding on an amount for the property, the interested parties bid on the interest rate they are willing to receive. The investor who bids the lowest rate wins the auction and is issued the tax lien certificate.

Once You've Bought a Tax Lien Certificate

After an investor places a winning bid for a specific tax lien certificate, a lien is placed on the property and a certificate is issued to the investor detailing the outstanding taxes and penalties on the property. Not all states, counties or municipalities offer tax liens. Some states, such as California, only perform tax sales on defaulted property, resulting in the winning bidder becoming the legal owner of the property in question.

The term of tax lien certificates typically ranges from one to three years. The certificate enables the investor to collect unpaid taxes plus the applicable prevailing rate of interest, which can range from 8 to more than 30 percent, depending on the jurisdiction.

The Rate of Return on Tax Lien Certificates

Spurred by the high state-mandated rates of interest, tax lien certificates may offer rates of return that are substantially higher than those offered by other investments. Tax liens generally have precedence over other liens, such as mortgages. If the property owner fails to pay the back taxes, the investor could potentially acquire the property for pennies on the dollar. Acquiring a property in that manner is a rare occurrence, since most tax liens are redeemed well before the property goes to foreclosure.

Associated Benefits and Risks of Tax Lien Certificates

Buying a tax lien certificate can, at times, prove to be an attractive investment. Some of the certificates have a low entry point, meaning you can buy some of them for a few hundred dollars. Compare that to a traditional investment like a mutual fund, which often come with a minimum investment requirement.

You also have the option to spread your money around, so you can buy multiple certificates for a low dollar value. And finally, the rate of return (as we mentioned above) is usually pretty consistent, so you're not going to have to worry about the ups and down of the market.

Negative aspects of tax lien certificates include the requirement for the investor to pay for the tax lien certificate in full within a very short period of time, usually one to three days. These certificates are also highly illiquid, since there is no secondary trading market for them. Investors in tax lien certificates also have to undertake significant due diligence and research to ensure that the underlying properties have an appropriate assessed value.

An example regarding the need for due diligence when researching tax lien certificates is a two-acre lot that may initially seem to be a good value, but it's actually a strip of land that is only 3 feet wide by 5 miles long. This renders the land unusable for many endeavors, such as building a home or a business.

VENDING MACHINE

The ads are alluring: "Make $500 an Hour in the Vending Business!" "Earn Money While You Sleep in a Vending Machine Business!" But they sound way too good to be true. Can vending machines really be a viable way to earn cash?

The National Automatic Merchandising Association reports that 18 percent of vending-machine operators make between $1 million and $5 million a year. But proceed with caution: The Better Business Bureau warns of scams, and a search of "vending machines" on the Federal Trade Commission's website unearths dozens of fines and lawsuits.

Here are a half dozen tips for getting into the vending-machine business safely and profitably.

1. *Decide on the vending machine type.*

Many vending machines are filled with a selection of drinks and snack foods. Others focus more narrowly on a particular category, such as ice cream, popcorn, cigarettes, videos (think Redbox), or personal hygiene. Some machines dispense individual units; others offer items in bulk, such as hard candy and gumballs.

2. *Get the proper licenses.*

In some states you'll need a seller's permit to operate vending machines, and many states require you to charge sales tax on the items in the machines. The tax varies by state, as does the minimum price that launches the requirement to collect the tax. Be sure to check with your local licensing office to find about the requirements in your area.

3. *Buy the machines.*

Decide whether you want to buy new or used machines. Prices can vary wildly: A new machine often runs a few thousand dollars, while used ones go for a few hundred or less on Craigslist, eBay, or Amazon. Keep in mind that all machines eventually break down, so you'll need to either hire someone to repair them or learn to do so yourself.

4. *Buy or lease a truck.*

Depending on how large your operation is, you'll need a van — or, perhaps, a specialized beverage truck — to carry products from machine to machine. A used truck starts at about $5,500 at places like Specialty Trux, or you can lease a basic truck for about $500 a month.

5. *Find a supplier.*

You can buy products in bulk at a local big-box store or go online. Check out sites like Candymachines.com for bulk candy, or SmartVending for a full line of supplies. Markups will vary, depending on the product. Bulk items, such as candy and gumballs can be marked up 200 to 300 percent, while single items can typically be marked up between 60 and 100 percent. Of course, the more products you buy, the better price you'll get, so you may have to settle for lower markups when just starting out in order to be competitive, and then increase them as you add machines.

6. *Secure a location or two.*

Where you place your vending machines will determine how successful you are. Check out each site before you approach its owner. Look for a place that gets a lot of foot traffic, such as an airport, a parking lot, a shopping mall, a large office building, or a busy waiting room. Once you select a location, approach the owner and work out a deal. Some vending machine operators offer the owner a small percentage of their profits; others donate a portion of sales to charity. It's also recommended that you sign a written contract whenever you place a machine.

7. *Service your machines.*

Once your machines are placed, it will be up to you to keep them clean, well-stocked, and in working order. You may be able to do this by visiting once a week, but if the machine is popular, you may need to turn up more often.

Of course, all of this isn't quite as easy as earning money while you sleep. But with careful planning, hard work, and a little luck, you can run a successful vending-machine business.

YOUTUBE CHANNEL

YouTube is currently the most powerful video-sharing platform in the world. Since its launch in 2005, it has produced numerous millionaires, with the highest-earning star pulling in $12 million in revenue in 2015 (Forbes). Plus, according to YouTube, the number of channels that hit six figures in annual earnings through the platform is doubling each year.

I've rounded up ideas from the pros to show you first how to make money on YouTube, plus some tips on how to make sure your channel is a success.

1. *Try to Make Videos That Don't Have Too Much Competition*

Find a topic where there aren't many other videos and then exploit it. For example, if you try to review tech gadgets, your video will be buried under the many other reviews that flood YouTube. But, if you make something more creative, like "15 Apps That Make You a Genius," chances are you will rank higher in searches in the relevant categories. Always try to find unexploited sub-niches within your niche on which you can create videos.

2. *Be Consistent with Your Videos*

YouTube is paying less and less for views these days. Fortunately, you can stack different business models to maximize your income. To start, focus on making as many high quality videos as you can and be regular in your schedule. These will need to be mostly reviews, advice and experience-based videos for this tactic to work. When you have lots of videos, you'll show up in all kinds of searches. Makes sure you enable ads on your page and then recommend affiliate products in your videos. To use this strategy, find a product on Amazon or Clickbank, review it in the video, then include a link in your description and make sure you tell people to click the link in the description. When they buy the product, you get paid a commission.

3. Create and Sell Information Products

If you know a professional skill, you can teach it to make money. If you are a graphic designer, you can teach graphic design. Even if you don't have a skill you can teach, you can learn a new skill quickly. And don't worry about not being an expert.

Once you know what skill you will be teaching, start creating free YouTube videos on the subject. For example, if you are good with Photoshop, make videos on how to edit pictures or design logos in Photoshop.

To get views on your videos, make a list of all the people who are making Photoshop tutorials. Once you do that, make another list of the top five videos of these competitors. All of these videos have been proven to work. If you make similar videos with similar titles and similar video tags, you have a very high chance of getting discovered.

Once you have at least five to six thousand YouTube subscribers, you can launch an information product. Basically, a premium video course on Photoshop where you teach your subscribers the basic. Because you have already helped your subscribers with the free videos, they will be likely to buy your video course.

4. Make Money with Video Blogs

With a video blog, you will generate income by creating work from your expertise. The video blog places you as a subject matter expert and people want to work with the best. When a viewer begins to need services around information you have already talked to them about, they will come to the experts first.

They may come to your YouTube channel for something that they cannot complete on their own. Now that you have provided them with advice on a topic, they complete the task successfully. They will now come back to you on bigger projects or smaller ones they don't have time for.

The nice thing about a video blog is it is for anyone in the services industry. You can be an auto mechanic, marketing agency, doctor/physician, in home improvement, and so on. Anyone who provides a service to a consumer can talk to show their expertise on topics.

People are doing much of their research prior to purchasing these types of services, so why not show the consumer your expertise and why they should buy your service over anyone else's. Buying a product is usually just price, but when buying a service, you want to know who you are working with.

5. Become a Bitcoin Expert on YouTube

Talking with my group of entrepreneurs, we have discovered that we have something in common: we all want to invest in bitcoin, but we do not know exactly how. Virtual currencies have become a revolutionary concept in the field of monetary transactions. But because the change was so abrupt, there is still a great lack of understanding about this new way of doing business.

It could be possible sell traffic to exchanges that buy and sell cryptocurrencies and then, if the channel reaches enough subscribers and visualizations go up, the main source of income would be the platform itself.

6. *Become a YouTube Partner*

Today, anyone whose account is in good standing can become a YouTube partner through expressly allowing YouTube to place advertising in, on, and around your video content. Google makes money from the views of these ads and partners can then earn a percentage via a Google AdSense account. Exactly how much money a partner can make varies enormously and depends on a range of different factors. Find out how to become a YouTube Partner in this article.

7. *License Your Video*

In a digital era where everyone can create and distribute media, the rules of engagement between the media industry and individuals seem ever more confusing. But once you have this down, it will be easy to start earning from your video's rights. You can either wait for media representatives to reach out to you about using your video, or you can upload it on a marketplace like Jukin. Find out all about video licensing in this article.

8. *Promote Your E-commerce Website Through YouTube Videos*

YouTube really is one of the most effective and cheapest ways to market your e-commerce store. People are highly visual and watching a video on what a product actually looks like, how easy it is to use, and how it can benefit them.

How other individuals have experienced good results with your brand (customer testimonials) can go a long way towards attracting more interest and attention, compared to the written text. This, in turn, can boost your sales in your online store. Read this article to learn how to sell products from a WordPress website.

9. *Create Reviews and Earn Through Affiliate Marketing*

I have found that reviewing products and offering people bonuses to buy from them through your link underneath the YouTube video is a great way to make money as an affiliate marketer using YouTube.

You can leverage the YouTube videos to get people to know, like and trust you, which makes it a lot easier to sell something. Plus, the built-in audience of YouTube, being the number two search engine on the planet, and the results which tend to rank highly on Google (since they own YouTube) help you naturally get traffic to your videos, which can bring in more profits for you.

10. *Promote Your Channel as a Brand and Sell Merchandise*

Once you build a good level of recognition and engagement with your audience, you can take it up a notch by establishing your channel as your own personal brand. You can sell branded merchandise, such as shirts, mugs, umbrellas, or items that are more relevant to your niche.

A good example of this is fitness guru Cassey Ho, who was able to turn her Blogilates YouTube channel into branded activewear, gym bags, sports bottles, etc.

11. *Start Teaching via YouTube Videos and Link Them to Your Paid Online Courses*

Share any business-related knowledge that you possess that isn't common knowledge for the average person but something they would likely pay to learn. Examples include how to leverage LinkedIn effectively for your small business, how to write blogs to get noticed by bigger publications, or something simple like accounting.

You can then easily create your online course on a site like Teachable—they will host your classes, provide all the payment gateways and everything else you need to run your business. All you have to do is get people there by advertising on places like YouTube, Google or Facebook. After that, the business runs completely on its own and you can collect monthly passive income.

12. *Manage YouTube Channels*

If you are knowledgeable about how to operate a YouTube channel and how to use the different features of the platform, you can work as a manager for an account. YouTube has added a feature wherein one account can be managed by several people.

It depends on your agreement with the account owner, but some of your functions could include uploading videos (you can use Hootsuite to schedule your posts), responding to and leaving comments, thinking of video ideas and titles, writing the video descriptions and including links, and promoting the videos on various social media platforms. You can create an account on freelancing platforms, such as Upwork or Fiverr, to offer your video creation and editing services.

13. *Buy Helpful Videos That People Will Want to Use and Resell Them*

To be able to update their channel regularly, some YouTube account owners may consider looking for existing videos that they can buy and post on their page. This provides an opportunity for experienced and creative videographers to sell their work. Webinars and video training courses are especially profitable and marketable.

You cannot sell your videos directly through YouTube, but you can promote through the platform by giving a sneak peek of what you do and then linking to where they can buy the full video.

14. *Post Sponsored Reviews*

YouTube allows sponsored content, but make sure that you comply with the site's terms and guidelines regarding videos of this nature. Keep in mind that companies are willing to pay you for your video reviews because of the high level of credibility that you have built with your followers, so be honest in your reviews and opinions. Do not push a product that you personally do not want to use.

Remember that your viewers would love to hear your real experience with the brand and not some sort of canned marketing pitch.

15. *Become a Freelance Video Creator/Editor*

Remember that making money on YouTube does not necessarily mean appearing in front of the camera. There are opportunities to work and earn income behind the scenes too. One way is by creating and editing videos for other people. This is similar to ghostwriting—you make the content based on your client's or employer's requirements, and then they post your work under their name.

Getting ghost workers is how successful people usually keep their YouTube channels and blogs updated in the midst of all their work commitments. You can market your video-making skills as a freelancer. Fit Small Business shares the ultimate guide on how to become a full-time freelancer.

16. *Have a Unique Personality and Capture Attention*

Here's a list of the commandments you need to follow to be successful on YouTube. These are the basics! Once you get more involved with YouTube, then you'll understand more about them:
- Make your profile and channel artistic
- Create a ritual with catchy phrases or slogans
- "Call to Action"—tell your viewers to subscribe
- Collaborate with other creators
- Create content based on the comments your fans write
- Come up with original and clever titles for your videos
- Make your thumbnail interesting—something that grabs people's attention
- Write descriptions with a hook—don't say too much or too little
- The most important thing: good image and audio

17. *Be Visible: Upload One Video per Week*

Upload a video at least once a week and let your subscribers know about it. Respond to their comments, let your fans get in touch with you, and build your fan base. Mention in advance when you're uploading a new video—date and hour, if at all possible. You need to fall in love with your project, and you need to be persistent. These things, like anything else, take time. Remember, no one gets to one million followers overnight.

18. *Channel Your Originality and Creativity*

Don't rehash other people's video content. Besides the possibility of getting your YouTube channel gutted for violating intellectual property rights, your audience will figure it out after a while and walk away.

19. *Focus on Something You Feel Passionate About and Don't Make It About the Money*

YouTube is like any other business: you need to be persistent and bring something new to the table. There are thousands of YouTube channels out there. The hugely successful ones are the ones who came first and who did it because they loved it, without expecting anything in return.

YouTube, like any other social media outlet, is about passion and doing it because you love to produce videos and you are creative. Making digital content is like that hobby that you need to turn into your daily work and maybe one day make a living from it.

20. *Use Your Available Tools and Equipment Before Investing in More Expensive Ones*

Start with your phone. Don't spend $5,000 to buy a 5D camera that you have no clue how to use. Your smartphone's camera is perhaps one of the best cameras out there—the trick is in the lighting.

With good lighting and your phone, you can produce something that could look almost as good as anything made by an award-winning director. Start simple and make it grow. It's like going to the gym: make it a habit and once you notice that you love it, get the equipment you need.

Final Words

Congratulations on making it to the end of this book, what an accomplishment! Hopefully, you have found at least one method that will work for you. Thanks for reading.

www.ingramcontent.com/pod-product-compliance
Lightning Source LLC
Chambersburg PA
CBHW051318220526
45468CB00004B/1404